insight text guide

Maude Ashton

We Have Always Lived in the Castle

Shirley Jackson

First published in 2022, reprinted in 2023, 2024, 2025.

Insight Publications Pty Ltd
3/350 Charman Road
Cheltenham VIC 3192
Australia
Tel: +61 3 8571 4950
Email: books@insightpublications.com.au

www.insightpublications.com.au

A catalogue record for this book is available from the National Library of Australia

Shirley Jackson's We Have Always Lived in the Castle / Maude Ashton

Maude Ashton asserts the moral right to be identified as the author of this work

ISBNs:
9781922771179 (print)
9781922771186 (digital)

Cover design by Melisa Paredes

Printed by Markono Print Media Pte Ltd

contents

CHARACTER MAP

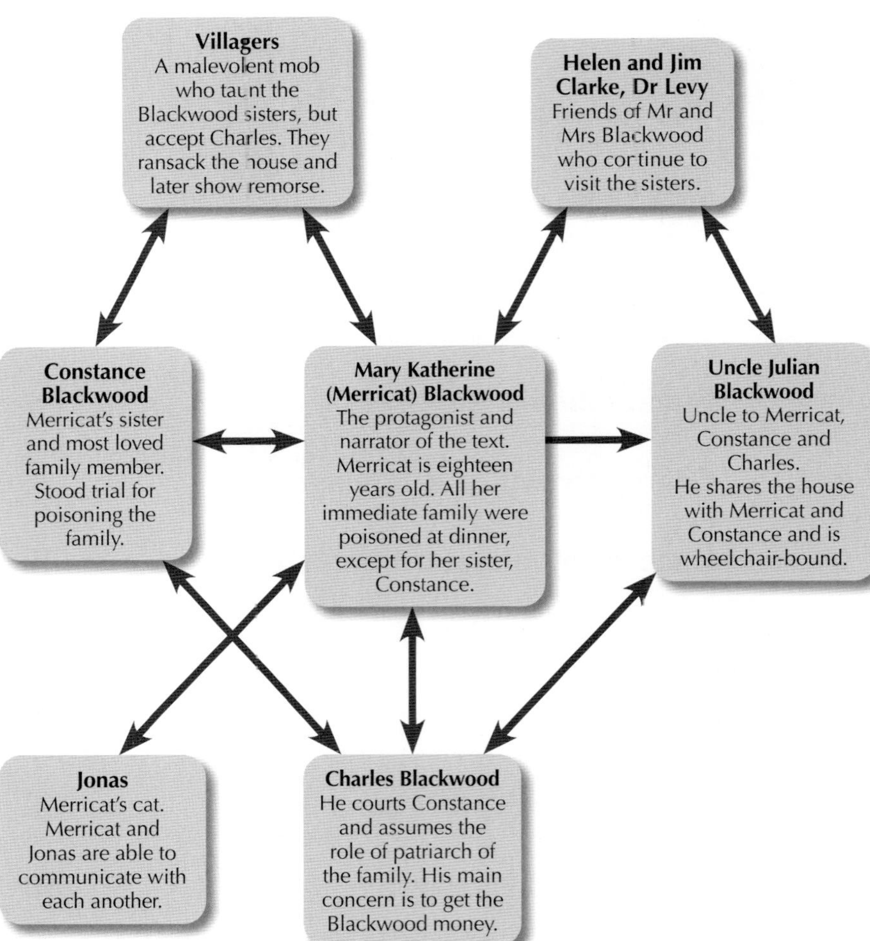

OVERVIEW

About the author

Shirley Jackson is a much-anthologised author in the United States, where her short story 'The Lottery' often appears on school syllabuses. Her last novel, *We Have Always Lived in the Castle*, attracted the greatest critical acclaim and was named one of the year's 'Ten Best Novels' by *Time* magazine when it was published in 1962.

Jackson was born into a prosperous middle-class family in California in 1919. Her mother described her as a 'wilful' child who had to have her own way and would spend hours in a fantasy land 'gawking at nothing'. Jackson's grandmother, Mimi, a Christian Scientist, also lived with the family. Mimi believed she could spiritually heal anyone who was sick by praying over them. Jackson's family background contributed to her showing an early aptitude for writing fiction and poetry, and her interest in the supernatural.

The family moved to Rochester, New York, in 1933. Jackson attended Syracuse University in New York, where she met her future husband, Stanley Hyman. Both Jackson and Hyman wrote for the college magazine and shared a love of literature that they pursued in their working lives after college. Hyman became an influential literary critic, while Jackson's fiction writing made her famous.

After graduating from university, Jackson married Hyman and they moved to Chelsea, New York, where Jackson began establishing her reputation as a writer, writing fiction for the prestigious *New Yorker* magazine, among others. The couple moved with their first child to North Bennington, Vermont in 1945. This New England town is often presumed to be the setting for her later novels, and several incidents with the townspeople in Bennington are thought to have provided the basis for her depiction of the villagers in *We Have Always Lived in the Castle*.

Jackson continued a rewarding writing career with the publication of 'The Lottery', her most famous short story; six novels and more than one hundred short stories followed.

James Frazer's *The Golden Bough,* a work that explores the intersection between magic and religion, was a strong influence on Jackson. Frazer, an eminent anthropologist in the twentieth century, researched myth and folklore, and the practices of sympathetic magic and contagious magic, all of which are instrumental in the creation of the character of Merricat.

Jackson died at forty-six years of age, in 1965, just three years after the publication of her critically acclaimed final novel.

Synopsis

Mary Katherine Blackwood (commonly called Merricat) and Constance Blackwood (also known as Connie) live in their childhood home with their Uncle Julian. The Blackwood house is just outside the village, but its fences and locked gates clearly emphasise the unfriendly nature of the relationship between the Blackwoods and the villagers.

Merricat notes that the library books on the kitchen shelf are five months overdue. She then recounts the day in late April, five months earlier, when she went to the village to get books and food. Merricat's trip to the village is highly planned so that she can avoid as much as possible the hostile villagers who, she says, have always hated the Blackwoods. The grocers serve her swiftly to get her out of the shop and she is conscious of unfriendly stares from the women there. At first it seems that Stella from the cafe is polite to Merricat, but two customers, Jim Donell and Joe Dunham, harass and bully her until Stella tells her to go home. During this trip Merricat wishes that the villagers were all dead; she imagines them rotting from within, and walking over their dead bodies.

Family friend Helen Clarke visits for tea, bringing her friend Mrs Wright with her. Uncle Julian recounts the night of the murders to Helen Clarke and Mrs Wright, explaining that the family was poisoned by arsenic in the sugar at dinner; he survived, disabled, because he took only a little sugar, and Constance was unharmed as she had no sugar at all. The visitors leave in a panic at the end of Uncle Julian's story.

The next day Merricat recognises omens of change and knows that trouble is on the way. This precedes the arrival of Charles Blackwood, cousin of Merricat and Constance and nephew of Uncle Julian. Cousin Charles finds his way into the house through the kitchen and sets about establishing himself as part of the family through his relationship with Constance.

As Charles further insinuates himself into the role of patriarch in the household it becomes clear to Merricat that his plans are not only to take her dead father's place, but to control the family money and banish Merricat and Uncle Julian. Charles has appropriated John Blackwood's bedroom and his place at the head of the table, symbols of the paterfamilias (male head of the household), and he begins to wear items of John Blackwood's clothing. Merricat escalates her plans to cleanse the house of Charles' presence and, excusing herself from the table, goes to his room, where she sweeps his pipe into the wastepaper basket, causing a fire.

Charles leaves to get help from the village and the firefighters eventually put out the blaze, observed by most of the villagers. A mob mentality overtakes the assembled crowd, and they destroy the contents of the house. Charles is among them and calls out for someone to get the safe (in which the family's wealth is apparently stored) out of the house, without knowing whether Constance, Merricat or Uncle Julian are alive or dead.

Feeling under threat, Merricat and Constance retreat to the woods and wait until the villagers disperse at the news that Uncle Julian has died in the fire.

Returning to the looted and destroyed house, the sisters make the kitchen their new home, shutting off the burnt upper storey. The kitchen has now truly become the heart of the house and the sisters retrieve provisions from the undisturbed cellar to provide themselves with food.

Helen and her husband Jim Clarke make several unsuccessful attempts to check on the sisters' welfare and to draw them out of the house, but the Blackwood women have closed off the front of the house and put cardboard over the windows to ensure their privacy. Dr Levy and Jim Clarke make another attempt to contact the sisters, who ignore their calls.

The villagers again begin using the shortcut through the Blackwood property to get to the highway, and children begin playing on the lawn at the front of the house.

Meanwhile Constance and Merricat continue to salvage what they can from the wreckage of the house and fashion a life with what remains. Constance makes clothes from tablecloths for Merricat and makes do with Uncle Julian's suits for herself. The village men begin to bring meals that their wives have cooked, leaving them outside the front door after dark. Cousin Charles makes one last visit, with a photographer in tow, but his hold on Constance is gone and they do not answer his knock.

Merricat and Constance sit beside the front door to observe the villagers and tourists who come and go, since their house has become a form of memorial or shrine. The novel ends with Merricat reporting that they are happy with this new life.

Character summaries

Mary Katherine 'Merricat' Blackwood

Merricat is the protagonist and narrator of the novel. She lives in 'the castle' of the title with her sister Constance and her invalid uncle, Julian. Merricat believes in omens and talismans and follows rituals; her constant companion is Jonas the cat. Merricat killed her mother, father, brother and aunt, and seriously injured her uncle, with arsenic poisoning. She is instrumental in burning down the house and setting up an alternative home in the kitchen with her beloved sister Constance.

Constance Blackwood

Constance is Merricat's older sister. She is spared from poisoning by Merricat because she is loving and kind towards her younger sister. Constance cooks and preserves food for Merricat and Uncle Julian, and later for Cousin Charles. She takes the blame for the poisonings in her sister's stead and is tried and acquitted, although the villagers still believe that she is the killer.

Uncle Julian

Uncle Julian is the brother of the now deceased John Blackwood, and uncle to Merricat, Constance and Cousin Charles. Uncle Julian is confined to a wheelchair, and spends most of his time recording the details he can remember from the night of the poisoning. He has moments of lucidity, but he is often muddled.

Cousin Charles

Cousin Charles is a gold-digging cousin of the Blackwoods. He comes to their house to obtain their money and property, possibly by marrying Constance and sending Uncle Julian and Merricat away. He is avaricious and cares little for the sisters or their uncle.

Helen and Jim Clarke

Helen Clarke is one of very few people who still enter the Blackwood house following the murders, coming for tea on Wednesdays. She persists in trying to persuade the young women to leave the burnt house after the fire. Jim Clarke is Helen's husband. He attempts to make the villagers leave when they are destroying the contents of the house after the fire.

Jim Donell

Donell is one of the worst aggressors from the village, who bullies and taunts Merricat at Stella's cafe. Donell is also the chief of the fire brigade, who leads the men in putting out the fire; ironically, he is then the first person to smash a window and lead the mob in destroying the house.

BACKGROUND & CONTEXT

1950s America

Jackson started writing *We Have Always Lived in the Castle* in 1960, when America had begun to redefine itself socially, economically and politically. Jackson had witnessed, throughout the 1950s, the rise and fall of McCarthyism (see below); indeed, she and her husband were themselves suspected of being communists and investigated by the FBI. She experienced the burden of the expectation that every woman should want to be a good housewife and the narrow strictures of this role. Jackson also made the transition from living in a city to moving to a satellite town, seat of highly conservative values and parochial attitudes. Jackson's lived experience of the 1950s provides a strong influence on the exploration of themes of exclusion, persecution, patriarchy and narrow-mindedness in *We Have Always Lived in the Castle*.

McCarthyism

McCarthyism is named after US Senator Joseph McCarthy who vigorously enforced a government-sanctioned crackdown against communists in the 1940s and 1950s. America and the Soviet Union, while not engaged in open conflict, remained hostile towards one another in what is known as the Cold War, and the government of the time instituted the House Un-American Activities Committee to find and expose communists and communist sympathisers. McCarthy believed communists had infiltrated government and that hidden communist spies were providing information to the Soviet Union that would undermine both the government and the American way of life. He used a Senate investigation committee to investigate any suspicious persons, opening the floodgates for rumour and suspicion to jeopardise the work and lives of anyone thought to have left-leaning sympathies. McCarthy brutally tracked and arraigned anyone who was rumoured to have progressive political views or whose life choices deviated from the norm. He instituted hearings in which people were interrogated for any 'suspicious' activity. Many people were tried, incarcerated or pursued for years by his team of investigators. Eventually, more than 10 000 people lost their jobs to what came to be known as the Red Scare, and an atmosphere of uncertainty and mistrust coloured the American consciousness.

During this time, Jackson and her husband were on an FBI watchlist and several of their writer friends lost their jobs and had to work under pseudonyms. Much of the 'trial by rumour' that Jackson critiques in *We Have Always Lived in the Castle* reflects the effects of McCarthyism on middle America. Jackson and Hyman were not the stereotypical 1950s American couple: Hyman was Jewish while Jackson was not; Jackson had a degree and was a successful writer; their friends were from multicultural backgrounds, including the Black writer, Ralph Ellison. They were not easily accepted in the small town of Bennington, where they lived for many years, and Jackson was ostracised by the community after taking issue with the way the school was run. In the McCarthy era these differences were magnified, making the family a target for gossip.

New England and witchcraft

In the 1690s in New England (where Jackson was living at the time of writing *We Have Always Lived in the Castle*) religious zealotry and isolationism intensified an already acrimonious atmosphere and eventually gave rise to accusations of witchcraft and trials by denunciation. A kind of mass hysteria swept parts of New England and everyday people became caught up in a real witch-hunt. Salem, New England, was already beset by arguments about property boundaries and land grants, there were simmering tensions between rival families, and outcasts from the community became the first victims once the witch trials began. Most affected by the accusations were women who did not 'belong', or who were seen to be different in some way. Once mass hysteria took hold, the witch trials began and 200 people were imprisoned, nineteen people were hanged and one man was 'pressed' to death.

The parallels between Merricat and Constance's position as outcasts who are hated by the locals and the historic victims of the Salem witch trials are numerous: the Blackwood women are isolated and reclusive; the villagers resent the Blackwood family's wealth; they are also aggrieved by the fence that delineates the Blackwood property from the village and prevents them taking a shortcut through the property to the highway; Constance has been tried for murder and is known for her remarkable knowledge of plants and poisons; and Merricat actually believes in magic, has a black cat as her familiar and practises, however fruitlessly, whatever magic she can using household objects.

Similarly, the connections between Jackson's villagers and the people of Salem in 1692–93 are striking. Salem's population was divided over issues of property boundaries and grazing rights, and the mood was ripe for accusations and retribution. The hunting of 'witches' and the trials that followed were the result of moral panic, or mass hysteria, among the people of Salem. The people of the unnamed village in New England where the Blackwoods live suffer from a similar kind of mass hysteria, isolating Merricat and Constance, gossiping about them, chanting accusatory rhymes and, eventually, wrecking their house and threatening to 'put them back in the house and start the fire all over again' (p.108) when they see that the sisters have escaped the flames. The mass hysteria is exemplified by the villagers' pursuit of Merricat and Constance across the grounds:

> For one terrible minute I thought that they were going to join hands and dance around us, singing ... They were trying not to touch us; whenever I turned they fell back a little. (p.108)

Women's roles

In the 1950s, women's roles were strictly defined; they were the homemakers, wives and mothers of the men who were creating wealth in the postwar era. Maintaining the house and nurturing the family were the primary duties for women in America, and these roles were reinforced by the lack of jobs for women once men returned from World War II, as well as by societal mechanisms such as advertising and the media. Indeed, the term 'nuclear family' arose at this time, indicating that the family was the building block upon which society was built, and it was the role of women to create and maintain that nuclear family. Women were almost solely responsible for cooking and cleaning the family home, while the men worked outside the home to earn money.

In *We Have Always Lived in the Castle*, Jackson addresses both the limitations of the socially sanctioned roles of women and the ways in which women transgressed societal expectations. It is clear that generations of Blackwood women have been solely responsible for the domestic duties in the house, evidenced by the collections of dinner settings that each Blackwood wife brings with her and the shelves of preserves in the cellar to which each wife contributes. At the end of the novel the two sisters retreat to the women's domain, the kitchen, to live on whatever can be gleaned from the cellar and the kitchen garden, in addition to the offerings left by the villagers. Jackson highlights the cracks in these gendered roles through the two main characters: Constance is the supreme housewife, although she has an impressive knowledge of poisons; Merricat imposes increasingly strict rules about what domestic items she can or cannot touch until her domestic connection becomes almost non-existent. Jackson emphasises the ambiguity of women's work in the house and the temporary nature of their achievements. For example, the preserves that are created by generations of Blackwood women, although beautiful and a 'poem' (p.42) to their existence, may be lethal if consumed.

The American Dream

The pervading ethos of the American Dream is that of upward mobility achieved through hard work. The American Dream posits that, regardless of class, education or background, each person can improve their lot in life, own a nice house, drive a big car and enjoy a better life than the generation before them.

In many ways *We Have Always Lived in the Castle* provides an antithetical statement to the American Dream; what began with generational wealth and the trappings of economic success is replaced by the bare bones of a house, no access to the outside world, and a life in which money is valueless. John Blackwood's legacy is reduced to ashes and the value of conspicuous consumption is revealed to be a useless mirage. Merricat and Constance live a constrained and reclusive life, but they have more freedom.

GENRE, STRUCTURE & LANGUAGE

Genre

Jackson is often described as a writer of horror or suspense fiction and much of her earlier work could be seen as belonging to that genre. *We Have Always Lived in the Castle* seems to fit more comfortably, but not exclusively, into the female Gothic genre. Gothic literature is considered to have begun with the publication of *The Castle of Otranto*, written by Horace Walpole in 1764, and it usually incorporates a number of recognisable elements. For example, in Gothic fiction the past often haunts the present, so Gothic novels are frequently set in medieval castles, towers or manors, meaning that the past is forever represented in the present to the people living there. The Gothic protagonist is usually haunted by something hidden, a mystery that is hinted at and eventually revealed. Often this protagonist is a naive, innocent female, whose parents may be dead and who is exposed to danger in some way. Another Gothic trope is of the mysterious stranger whose true identity is only revealed later in the plot and whose arrival creates disruption in the order of the house. Supernatural and inexplicable events and omens hint at the heart of the mystery, and Gothic fiction also contains themes of the grotesque, often involving characters whose mind or body is in some way deformed. Gothic novels also frequently include a sexually repressed character.

The origins of the female Gothic can be traced back to the works of female writers, such as Mary Shelley's *Frankenstein* (1818) and the novels of Ann Radcliffe, which were mostly published in the 1790s. The definition was later expanded to include novels that have elements of the traditional Gothic but incorporate a female protagonist who rejects the conventional roles of mother, wife and housekeeper. Gothic novels engender fear; in the case of the female Gothic, that fear is of entrapment within a domestic role and leads to a rejection of the patriarchy.

Structure

The traditional structure of a novel includes exposition that is interrupted by conflict. Rising action follows until the climax of the story, followed by falling action and a denouement, or resolution.

The exposition of the plot happens in the first paragraph on the first page of *We Have Always Lived in the Castle*, which opens with a succinct introduction from Merricat: 'My name is Mary Katherine Blackwood. I am eighteen years old, and I live with my sister Constance' (p.1). This efficiently establishes that this will be a story about Merricat and her sister Constance. The practical, forthright and confident introduction continues, but with some surprising observations from the protagonist: 'I have often thought that with any luck at all I could have been born a werewolf, because the two middle fingers on both my hands are the same length' (p.1). The confidence with which Merricat shares this bizarre notion, her disappointment that she is not a werewolf and her resignation to her human lot – 'I have had to be content with what I had' (p.1) – set up for the reader not only Merricat's otherness and her magical thinking, but also her determination to make do with what she has in order to achieve her ends. Merricat's list of the things she likes – 'my sister Constance, and Richard Plantagenet, and *Amanita phalloides*, the death-cup mushroom' (p.1) – foreshadow the poisonings that will only be revealed later in the novel. Constance is her only loved one and Merricat surprisingly follows her name with that of Richard Plantagenet, who was crowned King of England in 1483 after having assasssinated the two young nephews who had stood in his way. Together with the mention of the death cap mushroom, a deadly poisonous fungus, this lays the foundations for the revelations at the centre of the plot. The final sentence in the introduction is an outrageous juxtaposition with the references to poisons which immediately precede it, flatly stated in a tone typical of Merricat: 'Everyone else in my family is dead'. Merricat's introduction provides so much of the exposition of the novel in such a succinct and emotionless way that the reader is prepared, and intrigued, to follow all the leads that are laid out in the first paragraph.

Much in the same way that Jackson works the exposition through foreshadowing and allusion, the conflict that the introduction of Charles brings is presaged by Merricat's intuition that 'change was coming' (p.40). These elements of foreshadowing and allusion are important in the structure of the novel because Jackson builds suspense and uncertainty through these techniques; we are told what to expect in the revelation of the plot, but only in tangential ways. The atmosphere becomes uneasy with the approach of Charles. Jonas the cat is 'fretful' and 'running up a storm' (p.40). Merricat hears her dead family 'calling me' and thinks that they 'want me to get up' (p.40). These premonitions occur in Chapter Three but it is not until Chapter Five that Charles, after circling the house, makes his way inside and brings conflict to the Blackwood household. The conflict that he sparks replicates the conflict between the deceased members of the Blackwood family and Merricat. Charles' suggestion that Merricat be punished triggers memories of her family's punishments: '"Punish me?" I was standing then, shivering against the door frame. "Punish me? You mean send me to bed without my dinner?"' (p.94).

The climax of the novel – the burning of the house and the purgation of the male Blackwood legacy – is preceded by a similar foreshadowing in the abandoned summerhouse. Here, Merricat re-enacts a family dinner where she is praised, not scolded, by her family. Immediately following this revision of history, Merricat is instrumental in setting fire to the house, providing the climax of the action and a turning point in the plot of the novel.

The denouement or resolution is the banishment of Charles and the establishment of Merricat and Constance as mistresses of their own fate, with what remains of the burnt house now their castle.

Language

Narrative voice

The first-person narration and the mordant tone of the narrator work together to create much of the grim humour throughout the novel. While the reader may be horrified by some of Merricat's actions, our connection to her is strengthened by the fact that she is narrating the novel, so we are positioned to interpret events from her point of view. First-person narration creates a sense of intimacy between the narrator and the reader; we are given access to everything Merricat sees and feels. For example, Merricat tells us that her father's study had books covering two walls, but she borrows books from the library each week because she 'liked fairy tales and books of history' (p.2), which, clearly, are not in her father's study. This adds to our understanding of Merricat living on the periphery of the family. Equally, first-person narration is limited, and limiting to the reader; we are only given access to the things Merricat sees, feels and experiences, and must rely solely on her interpretation of events.

Merricat is an unreliable narrator – that is, her version of events should not be entirely believed by the reader. An unreliable narrator is usually a first-person narrator who is an untrustworthy storyteller, either because they intend to deceive the reader or because they are in some way misguided. In *We Have Always Lived in the Castle* the unreliable narrator is untrustworthy because she instinctively rebels against convention, and because her mental state is erratic. She poisons her family out of anger, being aggrieved at being sent to bed without dinner, and at not having the loving care that she wanted from the family. Merricat's unstable mental state is shown through physical symptoms that make her unable to speak or move. She sometimes feels as if she is bound and constricted and, at times of great stress, she is unable to see colour; everything she looks at is black and white. Merricat's magical thinking, isolated existence and belief in rituals, devices, omens and talismans separate her from any 'normal' life, but these characteristics become familiar to the reader over the course of the novel and Merricat's view develops a logic of its own. On a technical level, Jackson generates intrigue and suspense by creating ambiguity and doubt through Merricat's unreliable narration.

Tone

Despite the gruesome events of the novel, the narrator, Merricat, has a matter-of-fact and sometimes comic tone. When Helen Clarke and Mrs Wright come to visit, the tone is wholly humorous; as Helen Clarke clumsily makes her way across the room she 'jostled Mrs. Wright and sent Mrs. Wright sideways like a careening croquet ball off into the far corner of the room where she sat abruptly and clearly without intention upon a small and uncomfortable chair' (p.25). When Julian describes the murders to Mrs Wright he undercuts the seriousness of the crime with a comic misunderstanding of Mrs Wright's interjections:

> 'She should not have been doing the cooking,' said Mrs. Wright strongly.
>
> 'Well, of course, there is the root of our trouble. Certainly she should not have been doing the cooking if her intention was to destroy all of us with poison; we would have been blindly unselfish to encourage her to cook under such circumstances.' (pp.35–6)

When Mrs Wright again asserts that Mrs Blackwood, the mother, should have been doing the cooking, Julian replies with dry humour, 'I personally preferred to chance the arsenic' (p.36).

Symbolism – the house

The house in *We Have Always Lived in the Castle* is an ambiguous entity; it is both a residence and a monument to the Blackwood male lineage until it is burned down, then it becomes a ruined castle that is also an altar and a monument to the Blackwood women.

In the beginning the house is a metaphor for power and ownership as it is passed down from one male heir to another. Female offspring aren't given property in the patriarchal wills. (The Rochester house that belonged to Constance and Merricat's mother is sold to the junk dealer although it should rightfully belong to Constance.) When women marry into the family, they become known as the 'Blackwood women' and their individual stories are subsumed into the Blackwood narrative. Their role is to maintain the day-to-day operations of the household. For the Blackwood women, their legacy is stored away in the domestic background, in the cellar or the pantry. Merricat, in destroying and closing off parts of the house, creates a reclusive castle in its domestic periphery.

Symbolism – clothes

Clothes also symbolise power in this novel. When Charles attempts to become the patriarch of the family he begins to appropriate John Blackwood's clothes and jewellery, symbols of status and authority. Constance considers wearing her mother's rope of pearls, a token of respectability and middle-class prosperity. While Merricat, like Charles and Constance, still treats clothes as emblematic, she invests them with different, more arcane powers. Every Thursday Merricat retrieves 'their' (i.e. her dead family members') clothes from the attic and wears them, telling the reader that Thursday is her most powerful day (p.41).

When Julian dies and all the sisters' clothes are burned, Constance says she will wear Uncle Julian's clothes, which Merricat says are like 'wearing the skins of Uncle Julian'. Another important detail is that Merricat is not barefoot when she goes into the village; she wears her mother's old brown shoes. Each piece of clothing has, for Merricat, a remnant of the original owner within it, giving the clothing the power to re-create something of its owner when worn. In many ways, although confident, Merricat sees that she is vulnerable to perceived threats and so the clothing provides an element of protection. Merricat's real source of power is in the natural world so it is appropriate that she chooses 'a suit of leaves' (p.135) to summon this world's sympathetic magic.

CHAPTER-BY-CHAPTER ANALYSIS

Chapter One (pp.1–17)

Summary: *Mary Katherine 'Merricat' Blackwood goes to the village, as she does regularly on Fridays and Tuesdays. She takes a carefully planned walk to shop for food and borrow library books. She also makes sure to stop at Stella's cafe, where she is bullied and harassed. She tells the reader that the people of the village hate her family. The children chant a mocking rhyme about her family when Merricat passes on the way home and she wishes them all dead.*

Key point

The opening chapter establishes several key elements of the text. It introduces the first-person narrator and establishes the circumscribed landscape of the novel, which comprises the Blackwood house and grounds, and the path Merricat takes through the village. It also establishes the antipapthy between Merricat and the inhabitants of the village.

The first chapter of the novel is famous for its opening paragraph in which much is established about Merricat, her relationship to her sister and to the world, and her state of mind. Her list of things she likes and dislikes is eccentric and sinister, grouping together disparate people and adding poison into the mix. The reader simultaneously dreads, and yet is unsurprised by, the last sentence, 'Everyone else in my family is dead' (p.1). The affectless statement that her family is dead establishes Merricat's mordant character and, as Merricat is the narrator, establishes the tone for the rest of the novel.

The reader's sense of being off-balance is amplified by Merricat undermining our expectations; when she comes out of the library 'the sun was shining and the false glorious promises of spring were everywhere' (p.3), and later she walks into the 'bright, misleading sunshine of April' (p.6). The words 'false' and 'misleading' warn us that everything is not as it seems. Indeed, people are not to be trusted. Merricat casts a jaundiced eye over the villagers and their parochial, gossiping habits: 'In this village the men stayed young and did the gossiping and the women aged with grey evil weariness' (p.3).

Merricat, Constance and Uncle Julian occupy the Blackwood house, which is fenced in and protected with padlocks on the gates; only Merricat can go to the village, and only on specific days, when she treads a careful and circumscribed path through the 'grey' village (p.6) and its malicious inhabitants. Mr and Mrs Elbert, the grocers, and Mrs Donell, the fireman's wife, can barely tolerate Merricat's presence in the same shop. When Merricat forces herself to go into Stella's cafe 'out of pride' (p.11) she is bullied by Jim Donell, the Fire Chief, and Joe Dunham, the carpenter. The first chapter gives the reader the only detailed description of the village and its inhabitants, but it is worthwhile remembering that we only see the village from Merricat's point of view.

As she passes them, the village children chant a hectoring rhyme at Merricat:

> Merricat, said Connie, would you like a cup of tea?
> Oh no, said Merricat, you'll poison me.
> Merricat, said Connie, would you like to go to sleep?
> Down in the boneyard ten feet deep! (p.16)

The chant is designed to intimidate her and further embeds the widely held belief that Constance poisoned her family.

Q Do you think the villagers are as evil as Merricat describes them to be? Find evidence in the chapter to support your answer.

Chapter Two (pp.18–39)

Summary: *Merricat returns home through carefully locked gates that keep the villagers out. Constance, her sister, is housebound but comes as far as the end of the garden to meet Merricat. Uncle Julian, John Blackwood's brother, who uses a wheelchair, recounts some of* *the details of the night of the poisoning. Helen Clarke comes to visit, bringing Mrs Wright with her. Helen Clarke encourages Merricat to come out of the house and be more sociable. Prompted by Mrs Wright, Uncle Julian recounts in detail how the family was poisoned by arsenic in the sugar bowl and Constance was tried for the murders. The visitors leave in panic.*

Key point

There is a form of class warfare being conducted by the Blackwood family against the 'common' people who live in the village. In this chapter we are told that Mrs Blackwood (the mother of Constance and Merricat) insisted that her husband put up a fence to prevent the 'common' (p.19) people traversing the shortcut through the Blackwood property to the highway. Mrs Blackwood herself came from a house in the village, the Rochester house (which is now dilapidated and owned by the junk collector, Harler), so her reasons for keeping the villagers out become more mysterious.

The fence is one of the sources of tension between the villagers and the Blackwoods, but the reader does not know what caused the fence to be put up, only that it was 'before' (p.19). Merricat remembers this time 'before' as a child when she imagines that 'the good people, the clean and rich ones dressed in satin and lace' came 'rightfully' down the driveway to visit, and the villagers used the path 'sneaking and weaving and sidestepping servilely' (p.18). Jackson clearly shows the mutual animosity between the villagers and the Blackwoods, but the Blackwoods' obvious sense of superiority is surprising in its virulence. When Constance remarks that someday she would go to the village, Merricat is 'chilled' (p.21) and this scene marks a turning point in the novel; Constance's statement is a catalyst for the events that follow.

Uncle Julian recounts some of the events from the night of the poisonings, saying that he overheard Mr and Mrs Blackwood quarrelling 'hatefully', with John Blackwood saying, 'We have no choice' (p.22). Once again Jackson uses ambiguity, this time through the half-heard conversation, to heighten suspense and tension. 'We have no choice' is a dramatic statement, but what do they have no choice in?

Helen Clarke comes to visit, bringing Mrs Wright, 'the frightened one' (p.25), with her. Jackson again uses comedy to tell the story of something quite horrific:

> And poor, poor Mrs. Wright, tempted at last beyond endurance, was not able to hold back any longer. She blushed deeply, and faltered, but Uncle Julian was a tempter and Mrs. Wright's human discipline could not resist forever. (p.31)

The comedic depiction of the characters of Mrs Wright and Helen Clarke has two effects on the narrative: it compounds the dry wit in the narrative voice that works throughout the novel, insisting that death can be interrogated for humour just as well as any other subject, and it also undercuts Helen Clarke's injunctions to Constance to 'come back into the world' (p.27). Mrs Wright has been brought by Helen Clarke precisely for this purpose; she would like to give 'a little luncheon' (p.27), which Constance would attend. Merricat takes swift revenge, smashing the milk jug, and frightening Mrs Wright further with the offer of 'Sugar?' (p.28), the very substance that Constance supposedly laced with arsenic to kill her family. Uncle Julian relates the events of the murders to Mrs Wright, much to the chagrin of Helen Clarke, who interrupts with, 'There is such a thing as good taste, Julian.' Jackson has Julian reply with a witty wordplay: 'Taste, madam? Have you ever tasted arsenic?' (p.31). Constance and Merricat share the 'merriment' as Mrs Wright is simultaneously frightened and mesmerised by Uncle Julian. As Mrs Wright becomes more engrossed in the details of the murders all three members of the family join in the comedy. Mrs Wright asks why Constance bought arsenic, Uncle Julian and Constance tell her it was to kill rats, and Uncle Julian explains: 'The only other popular use for arsenic is in taxidermy, and my niece could hardly pretend a working knowledge of that subject' (p.37). The visitors leave distraught and Constance tells Uncle Julian his performance was 'superb' (p.39).

Q Why do the Blackwoods toy with the visitors in this scene? What does this tell us about Merricat, Constance and Uncle Julian?

Chapter Three (pp.40–50)

Summary: *Merricat senses a change coming through the fretfulness of the members of the household, including Jonas the cat. Merricat's strict routines continue as she helps Constance in the house. Uncle Julian is visited by the doctor and reminisces about being indebted to John Blackwood for allowing Julian and his wife to live in the Blackwood house.*

Key point

Merricat's premonitory fear that a 'change was coming' (p.40) is held in check by the strict routines of running the house, where everything remains constant.

On Mondays the sisters neaten the house, Tuesdays and Fridays are shopping days, on Wednesdays Merricat checks the fences, on Thursdays she goes to the attic and dresses in 'their' clothes, on Saturdays she helps Constance, on Sundays she checks her 'safeguards' (p.41) – a box of silver dollars, a doll, a book nailed to a tree, six blue marbles, and her baby teeth. All of these routines are safeguards for Merricat, too, as they help to keep her from thinking about the thing she is most frightened of: 'them'. Merricat uses the pronouns 'they' and 'them' instead of the names of the deceased family members because she thinks that naming them will make them real. Constance, too, cooperates in erasing the family when Merricat is becoming anxious. Merricat wakes and tells Constance, 'I thought I heard them calling me this morning'. Constance immediately distracts her from this thinking by answering, 'Hurry with your breakfast … It's another lovely day' (p.41). These routines, rituals and distractions help in managing Merricat's anxiety just as her reliance on the supernatural helps her both to explain and to retaliate against perceived threats.

Appearances, suggests Jackson, can be deceptive. Two of the most important settings in this chapter, and in the text as a whole, are the kitchen, 'the heart of our house' (p.55), and the cellar, which contains the preserves made by generations of Blackwood women. The image of the preserves, 'deeply colored rows of jellies and pickles and bottled vegetables and fruit, maroon and amber and dark rich green, stood side by side in our cellar … a poem by the Blackwood women' (p.42), is one of the most lyrical passages in the novel. Yet, immediately following this lyrical description of the food, in typical sardonic style Jackson undercuts the image: 'Constance said it would kill us if we ate it' (p.42). Similarly, Uncle Julian, while fussing about being accurate with his notes, wants to entrust them to 'some worthy cynic who will not be too concerned with the truth' (p.43). Jackson's sly humour suggests that even the things we most value, our most highly prized possessions, may have hidden traps in them that make them worthless or even dangerous.

Q Why do the sisters follow such strict routines in the house?

Chapter Four (pp.51–8)

Summary: *Merricat roams the grounds with Jonas who, apparently, speaks to Merricat and tells her 'cat stories' (p.53). One of the important talismans, a book nailed to a tree, falls from its place and Merricat sees this as ominous. Constance shivers and Merricat cannot breathe as Cousin Charles comes closer to the house. When Charles enters the house, Merricat attributes his intrusion to the failure of the talisman. Merricat finds solace in the trees and the outdoors.*

Key point

This chapter culminates in the arrival of Cousin Charles, whose intrusion has been foreshadowed by the omens in the previous two chapters. Jackson builds suspense and wariness of Charles' arrival through repetition of the metaphor of 'the change' that was advancing on the household; the 'uneasy' weather (p.51); the nest of baby snakes Merricat finds and kills; and, finally, her father's notebook, which had fallen from the tree.

John Blackwood's notebook reveals more about his character and why the villagers may have had reason to dislike him, as it contains lists of those who owe him money or imagined favours. Jackson builds the tension of Cousin Charles' approach using language borrowed from the lexicon of mystery and crime novels. The ambiguous pronouns 'they' and 'he' are not attached to any particular characters, so the fear surrounding them is pervasive and insidious. The feeling of encroaching evil intensifies as Charles circles the house, looking for, and eventually finding, a way in.

We learn in this chapter that Merricat was, indeed, sent to an orphanage while Constance was on trial. Until now we have only had Uncle Julian's obviously addled recollection that Merricat died in an orphanage. Jackson leaves the reader with another mystery in this development: why does Uncle Julian think Merricat is dead when she lives in the same house as him, and why do they not speak to each other? Merricat, as usual, retreats to the woods and the creek to seek refuge in nature.

Q Give some examples of the ways in which Jackson employs foreshadowing to create an atmosphere of menace around Charles' arrival.

Q Can you explain why Uncle Julian thinks Merricat is dead? How does this affect our understanding of Merricat's character?

Chapter Five (pp.59–73)

Summary: *Charles Blackwood settles in very quickly to the patriarchal role, sleeping in the father's bed and engaging Constance in conversations about the future. Constance explains to Merricat that Charles' long absence from the family was because his father, Arthur Blackwood, forbade him from having contact with the rest of the Blackwood family.*

Key point

A major theme further developed in this chapter relates to the depiction of the house as both a 'castle' and a domestic sanctuary. Constance and Merricat spend their happiest and most productive times in the kitchen, but their rituals include neatening the whole house and maintaining it as a kind of memorial to their parents. The word 'neatened' (p.41) is deliberately chosen for their work in the house because it implies restoration to the original, whereas cleaning the house would remove traces of the earlier Blackwoods.

Merricat finds consolation in nature, retreating to one of her hiding places near the creek, where she has constructed a kind of nest, with 'leaves and branches for a bed'. Lying there with Jonas, Merricat feels protected, secure in the belief that there is, in fact, 'no change coming' and that everything 'would always be the same' (p.53). She returns to the house feeling protected and settled. Merricat combines this faith in nature with an escapist fantasy of living on the moon, which Constance indulges, but modifies. When Merricat declares, 'Today my winged horse is coming and I am carrying you off to the moon and on the moon we will eat rose petals', Constance counters, 'Some rose petals are poisonous' (p.59). In her mind Merricat has used a similar kind of 'wishing away' with Cousin Charles as she does with her fantasy of living on the moon. However, in Charles' case, although she has dismissed him as a ghost, tellingly, she believes that he is a ghost 'that could be driven away' (p.61), thus foreshadowing Charles' fate.

Once more Uncle Julian presents nuggets of truth, the 'tiny sparkling things' (p.62) inside his rambling, comic memories and plans.

> 'I really think I shall commence chapter forty-four,' he said, patting his hands together. 'I shall commence, I think, with a slight exaggeration and go on from there into an outright lie. Constance, my dear?'
>
> 'Yes, Uncle Julian?'
>
> 'I am going to say that my wife was beautiful.' (p.62)

The reader is in familiar territory in this passage, in which Jackson creates ambiguity through the characters' flawed recollections, escapist imaginings and intimations of danger. Uncle Julian's teasing conversation with Cousin Charles continues to play with the truth of the murders of the family: 'Charles is intrepid. Your cooking, although it is of a very high standard indeed, has certain disadvantages' (p.65). Jackson deftly works at the liminal edges of reality through the major and the minor characters in the novel, causing the reader to doubt the narrator and find very skewed authentication of events in the minor characters' recollections.

Cousin Charles continues to assume a patriarchal role by taking the father's seat at the dinner table, and giving unasked-for advice about how the family should handle their money.

Q Which of the main characters (Merricat, Constance, Uncle Julian or Charles) tells the truth most reliably? Provide evidence from the chapter to support your answer.

Chapter Six (pp.74–85)

Summary: *Charles goes into the village to do the shopping instead of Merricat. She takes the opportunity provided by Charles' absence to search the bedroom that was once her father's, and is now occupied by Charles, to find a 'device' (p.76) to use against him. Charles becomes increasingly threatening to Merricat and influential over Constance. Constance begins to berate herself for hiding from the world, and hints that she might be preparing to marry Charles.*

Key point

Charles further intrudes into the lives of the surviving Blackwoods, with a veiled threat to marry Constance and expel Merricat: 'What would poor Cousin Mary do if Constance and Charles didn't love her?' (p.78).

The reader's first introduction to Charles is as he circles threateningly around the outside of the Blackwood house. In this chapter he now circles closer and closer to his objective of taking over the patriarchal role of head of the household. Charles quickly assumes a position of dominance and the accoutrements of the patriarch in the household, despite having no right to be there. He sleeps in John Blackwood's bed, sits at the head of the table and questions the young women about their money and how they manage it.

Jackson shows how easily the women's security in their own home is breached by the arrival of Charles, who simply assumes he has authority because he is a man. He immediately undoes the protective power of the fence around the house: 'Constance gave him a key, perhaps our father's key' Merricat tells us, the result of which is that 'the house was not secure' (p.74). He next assumes control of their finances by issuing a warning that 'women alone like you are, you shouldn't keep money in the house' (p.74). Charles continues to undermine the women's control by doubting the accuracy of Constance's shopping list: 'Are you sure you put everything down?' (p.74). In this way Charles undermines their security and authority in their own domain and begins to destabilise the relationship between Constance and Merricat.

Merricat's response to Charles' disruption is to remove herself from reality and take comfort in fantasy and magic; she conjures the dream-life of the moon where 'all the locks are solid and tight' (p.75), and imagines Constance to be an old witch creating a gingerbread house. This is a reference to the Hansel and Gretel folk tale by the Grimm brothers, in which an old witch creates a gingerbread house to lure children for her to eat; Merricat casts Constance as the old witch and Cousin Charles as the prey. Merricat follows this with another story in which the locus of power is in herself, suggesting that Constance 'might make a gingerbread man, and I could name him Charles and eat him' (p.75). While these stories may seem escapist and fantastic, Merricat's intention to rid the house of Charles is deadly serious. Her next step is to rifle through her father's – now Charles' – room looking for 'something from this drawer [which] might be extraordinarily powerful, since it would carry a guilt of Charles' (p.76). She hangs a retrieved watch-chain from a tree to cast a hex on Charles.

Charles has some success in driving a wedge between Constance and Merricat by making Constance feel guilty for allowing Uncle Julian and Merricat to 'hide' with her from the public gaze (p.82). In addition to this, Charles further excludes Merricat by seeming to fit in with the villagers and joining them in making the women outsiders. As Merricat reflects, 'If I went into the village shopping again Charles would be one of the men who watched me going past' (p.81).

Patriarchy works hand in hand with misogyny as Charles gains more power and joins forces with the villagers in framing Constance and Merricat as dangerous and endangered outsiders, while Charles, despite being a Blackwood, can fit in with ease among the men in the village.

Charles' deceitful character does not escape Uncle Julian, however, who declares to Constance that Charles is a 'dreadful' young man from a corrupt family: 'He is dishonest. His father was dishonest. Both my brothers were dishonest … He is a bastard' (p.83).

Q How does this chapter further develop Charles' character? Support your answer with evidence from the chapter.

Chapter Seven (pp.86–96)

Summary: *Merricat puts garden waste in Charles' room and pours water on his bed. Charles retaliates by demanding to know how Merricat will be punished. Merricat suffers a psychological shock and reimagines the last family dinner with the family praising her instead of punishing her.*

Key point

In this chapter Jackson uses doubling and mirroring to show how Charles is attempting to re-create the patriarchal order, once presided over by John Blackwood, that Merricat and Constance had dismantled.

A fundamental aim of patriarchy is to wield economic power and, since men are in a privileged position at the top of the hierarchy, to maintain the status quo by controlling those with less power. Jackson often uses doubling to expose traits or secrets that characters try to hide. This occurs frequently through Uncle Julian's faulty memory. In this chapter, Uncle Julian confuses Cousin Charles with John Blackwood, Constance and Merricat's father. Uncle Julian addresses Charles using John's name: 'You are a very selfish man, John, perhaps even a scoundrel, and overly fond of the world's goods; I sometimes wonder, John, if you are every bit the gentleman' (p.92). While Uncle Julian appears to be confusing people with each other, what he says is equally true of Charles, whose intention of taking the young women's money is transparent. Charles becomes incensed when he discovers the buried money; he carries the silver dollars he retrieves 'tenderly' and shouts, 'It's not her [Merricat's] money' (p.88), when clearly it is.

At the height of Charles' anger he shakes the box of silver dollars so hard they threaten to fall and Merricat muses that she 'would like to see Charles on the ground, scrabbling after my silver dollars' (p.88). His avarice is shocking for Constance and Uncle Julian to see, and this scene marks the undoing of Charles' plan to become the head of the household as the victims of his scheme now see him for what he truly is. Merricat regains her equilibrium and comments coolly on the rat-like quality of Charles' furious ranting: 'I wondered how long Charles was going to go on shouting … his voice was getting thinner and higher; perhaps if he shouted long enough he would squeak' (p.90).

Merricat sees Charles as a combination of ghost and demon, and interprets his fit of anger and loss of status as 'the first twistings and turnings of the demon caught' (p.94). Charles' final attempt to control

Merricat – 'Aren't you even going to punish her?' (p.94) – triggers a memory of a familiar chastisement from her family, when she had been sent to bed without dinner. Merricat summons a picture of the last night that all members of her family were alive and seated around the dinner table, but she changes the dialogue into praise for her. In doing this, Merricat gains greater equilibrium and prepares to undertake the next part of her plan to rid the house of Charles.

Q In what ways does Charles resemble John Blackwood?

Q Why does Merricat choose the summerhouse to re-enact the family dinner?

Chapter Eight (pp.97–110)

Summary: *Merricat goes upstairs to what is now Charles' bedroom and sweeps his pipe into the wastepaper basket. A fire begins in Charles' bedroom and Charles' first concern is to get the money out of the house. He runs to get help from the village, and the villagers gather around the house, chanting and watching the blaze. Then, led by Jim Donell, they smash the windows and begin destroying the contents of the house. Constance and Merricat narrowly escape the marauding villagers while Jim Clarke and Dr Levy disperse the mob. Constance reveals that she knows that Merricat poisoned the Blackwood family.*

Key point

We cannot know whether Merricat deliberately starts the fire in the bedroom, but we can be sure that the instruments of the fire – Charles' pipe and matches, and the inherited family saucer he used for an ashtray – are powerful symbols of Charles' claim over the Blackwoods' domain, which Merricat has vowed to destroy.

Charles' shouting and ranting against Merricat fill the house in the same way as the smoke from his pipe. Just like the hated pipe smoke that permeates the house, Charles has insinuated himself into every part of the life of the house and assumed the position of paterfamilias. Charles has symbolically usurped part of the dowry of past Blackwood wives; the pervasive smoke of the pipe, which also leaves burn holes in the sitting room, and the saucers taken from their rightful storage place and scattered throughout the house are emblematic of Charles' infiltration of the domain of the young women and his assumption of control. His intrusion into even the historical sanctuary of the Blackwood women, the kitchen and pantry, and their dowry (each Blackwood bride brought a new china set with their dowry) is as shocking as his manners are crude. The saucers, Constance says, 'were from a set older than any I remembered' and 'come from a time before I was in the kitchen' (p.99); Charles' use and redistribution of them thus interrupts the historical rituals of the matriarchy.

Once the fire catches hold and Charles begins to panic, the tone of Merricat's discourse becomes cool and humorous once more. When Constance says, 'Charles – your pipe –', sending Charles running up the stairs, Merricat innocently wonders, 'Would it start a fire?' (p.101). When Charles screams at the sight of the fire from upstairs, 'with the exact sound of a bluejay in the woods', Merricat responds with dark humour: '"That's Charles," I said politely to Constance' (p.101). As Charles further reveals his avarice, piggish manners and loathing of Uncle Julian and Merricat, his status is diminished and Merricat regains her power. His first thought is to save the money from the fire: Jackson has him comically call to Constance, 'Don't try to carry the safe' (p.101).

Constance imbues the house itself with a personality that must be appeased when she says, 'We neatened it just the other day … It has no *right* to burn' (p.102). However, the humour melts away with the escalation of both the fire and the rage of the mob. Jim Donell, the leading instigator of the bullying and harassment of the Blackwoods, now appears as leader of the fire brigade, wearing 'a hat proclaiming him "Chief"' (p.104). The badge that Donell wears is also a symbol of male power and authority, and Jackson explores the legitimacy and ambiguity of that power when Donell, once the fire is out, carefully removes the hat with its badge and initiates the destruction that the mob has been baying for. Donell is both an authority figure and an agent of the status quo; beneath the tokens of legitimate power lie the same malicious forces that the mob represents.

The violence of the villagers once they become a mob is anonymous and incremental. What starts as 'a woman's voice' that is 'raised above the others' (p.104) becomes a shout of anonymous malice – 'Let it burn' – before being joined by the voices of more unnamed members of the mob declaring, 'Should of burned it down years ago' (p.105). When the senseless destruction of the house begins, initiated by Donell, the crowd then uses the familiar 'rhythmic and insistent' chant that Merricat recounts in the first chapter (p.106). By the time Dr Levy asks about the whereabouts of Julian, the mob is in a kind of trance and the answer a woman gives him, 'Down in the boneyard ten feet deep' (p.107), is a response to the hateful rhyme, not the question. The smashing, intimidation and violence escalate as the villagers, hardly recognisable now as individual people but acting in a shared crazed frenzy, surround the young women threateningly. Charles hysterically calls for the safe to be saved, and when Jim Clarke brings the mob to order by telling them that Julian Blackwood is dead inside the house, Charles calls, 'Did she kill him?' (p.109). Jackson thus confirms Charles as part of the mob, money-grabbing, and already persuaded that one of the girls, or both, is a killer.

Merricat's mental retreat into fairytale and folklore – 'I would cover her with leaves, like children in a story' – and dissociation from reality – 'Someday we would go to the moon' (p.110) – help her to recover once more from an attack against her and her sister. But lucidity comes as Constance confirms that she knows that Merricat poisoned their family, and Merricat acknowledges that it is true.

Q Why is it so significant that Jim Donell carefully removes his 'Chief' helmet before smashing the window?

Q How does this scene connect with the Salem witch trials? See the 'Background and context' section for more information on these trials.

Chapter Nine (pp.111–31)

Summary: *Constance and Merricat return to the house to find its contents smashed and ruined. The fire has destroyed the upper part of the house and the villagers have broken everything they could find downstairs. The sisters clean the debris from the kitchen and set up their living quarters there. Helen and Jim Clarke, and later Dr Levy and Jim Clarke, make attempts to communicate with the young women but to no avail.*

In this chapter the house makes a transition into the 'castle' of the novel's title. The fire, having destroyed the upstairs part of the house, now opens it up to the sky; the villagers have smashed almost everything inside and thus destroyed the generational power of the acquisitions that have held Constance and Merricat in thrall. Merricat recounts:

> I stood at the foot of the stairs, looking up, wondering where our house had gone, the walls and the floors and the beds and the boxes of things in the attic … I could feel a breath of air on my cheek; it came from the sky I could see, but it smelled of smoke and ruin. Our house was a castle, turreted and open to the sky. (p.120)

While Helen Clarke circles the house (reminding the reader of the menace of Charles' approach), beating on the kitchen door to be let in, the sisters hide from her, but this time with self-assurance and equanimity: 'Constance sighed, and tapped her fingers irritably and almost noiselessly on the stair rail. "I wish she'd hurry," she said into my ear, "my soup is going to boil over"' (p.123). The sisters now have the remains of the ruined house to themselves and they confidently forsake any social contact: 'We are going to lock ourselves in more securely than ever' (p.117).

Q How do you view the sisters' decision to lock themselves in? Is this their only option?

Chapter Ten (pp.132–46)

Summary: *Children from the village use the front lawn to play games and the villagers resume their use of the shortcut through the property. Constance improvises outfits from the clothes in Uncle Julian's room, and Merricat wears tablecloths. Merricat barricades the sides of the house to prevent people from getting to the kitchen where the sisters now live. Charles brings a photographer to the house and tries to lure Constance into opening the front door. Merricat and Constance are happy with the way that they now live but they have earned a reputation for being witch-like recluses.*

As Merricat and Constance become more reclusive, the house that they live in becomes more and more like a castle, with vines growing over the ruined roof.

While John Blackwood was alive the family was disliked but tolerated by the villagers, but in the absence of a patriarch the two women become objects of hatred. They are gossiped about, chanted at and treated as pariahs. Their house is destroyed and they are denigrated as witches and 'two old maids' (p.143). The sisters' own acceptance of their otherness is expressed through their happiness in their isolation, and in their descriptions of other people as 'strangers' (p.132); the villagers reject them because of that very otherness, so that they are also feared, ostracised and victimised because they do not comply with the norm.

Jackson's writing often deals with ambiguities and uncertainty, magic and illusion. In this final chapter of the novel, when the characters reinvent themselves not only as survivors but as pioneers of a new way of life, they divest themselves of their everyday clothes and take on other appearances. Constance wears Uncle Julian's shirts and suits, which Merricat describes as 'wearing the skins of Uncle Julian', telling her sister that 'Robinson Crusoe dressed in the skins of animals' (p.137). The symbolic connection between creating a new world to live in, free from the patriarchal order enforced by John and Charles Blackwood, and the reference to Robinson Crusoe reinforces the notion of a new world being created by the sisters.

Merricat chooses a symbolic suit for herself. She says, 'I will weave a suit of leaves. At once. With acorns for buttons' (p.135), a reference to the Green Man of folklore who dressed in oak leaves and acorns and represented rebirth and rejuvenation. In the seventeenth century the Green Man was used in pageants as a 'whiffler' who would clear the crowds away. Merricat chooses this 'suit of leaves' because of her affinity with the natural world but, symbolically, the Green Man costume also marks the beginning of a new life for the sisters, and a period of regeneration.

The villagers begin to bring food to the house after dark, apologising for the damage that they have done. The sisters recognise that the food is a kind of religious offering: 'We are the biggest church supper they ever had' (p.139). But the villagers are also attempting to appease the women in the house, whom they suspect might be vengeful witches. The house takes on many new identities: it is now a 'castle', a monument to the women who live there, and a fearful place where offerings are made to placate the inhabitants. When a local boy tearfully chants the old rhyme at their doorstep on a dare, that night they find 'on the doorsill a basket of fresh eggs and a note reading, "He didn't mean it, please"' (p.146).

The novel ends in a recognisably wry, ambiguous tone, with the women joking about cooking and eating a child. But it is Merricat who has the last word: '"Oh, Constance," I said, "we are so happy"' (p.146).

Key point

In this final chapter Jackson further explores the ways that a community rejects and ostracises those who are different from the norm, particularly when they are women, motivated in part by fear.

CHARACTERS & RELATIONSHIPS

Mary Katherine 'Merricat' Blackwood

Key quotes

'I like my sister Constance, and Richard Plantagenet, and *Amanita phalloides*, the death cup mushroom. Everyone else in my family is dead.' (p.1)

'On Sunday mornings I examined my safeguards, the box of silver dollars I had buried by the creek, and the doll buried in the long field, and the book nailed to the tree in the pine woods; so long as they were buried where I had put them nothing could get in to harm us.' (p.41)

'… bow your heads to our beloved Mary Katherine, I thought, or you will be dead.' (p.111)

Mary Katherine Blackwood, known as Merricat, is the protagonist of *We Have Always Lived in the* Castle and she narrates the events of the novel. As narrator, Merricat interprets for the readers the events and characters in the novel, and Jackson intends the experience of reading her narrative to be a disturbing one. Merricat is driven by the need to wrest power from anyone who tries to dominate her; her thoughts are full of killing sprees and revenge, alternating with escapist fantasies of living on the moon with her beloved sister, Constance. Although she is eighteen during the events she describes, she often acts in a childish way: not wanting to wash, smashing crockery, running away and hiding. Merricat also seeks to control the world around her using magic, safeguards and tokens to ward off outsiders.

Merricat sees the world as hostile and 'full of terrible people' (p.54) whom she must defend herself against, but she knows that she has no status in that world and therefore no power. Merricat was an outsider even within her own family, who punished her regularly by sending her to bed without dinner. Constance tells Helen Clarke, 'Merricat was always in disgrace … She was a wicked, disobedient child' (p.34). The reader can gather that her family rejected Merricat even from an early age, and she responded by trying to make herself feel safe using magic, finding and burying things 'even when I was small' (p.41). We learn that these things included her 'baby teeth', which she hoped one day 'would grow as dragons' (p.41). In this fantasy she depicts herself, even as a child, like an embattled mythological hero.

If Merricat's family did not provide security for the admittedly strange child, then certainly there was no other source of comfort for her in the community in which she lived. The Blackwood family saw themselves as superior to the villagers, a view shared by Merricat, and the villagers viewed the Blackwoods as entitled and money-hungry. After the murders of the family members and Constance's trial, this animosity turned into something much more malicious as the villagers became convinced that Constance was a murderer, despite her being acquitted by the court.

Merricat unashamedly tells the reader of her disgust for the villagers. In her imagination she sees them rotting and their houses decaying. She hates their 'flat grey faces with the hating eyes' (p.8) and would like to see them all dead: 'I would have liked to come into the grocery some morning and see them all, even the Elberts and the children, lying there crying with the pain and dying' (pp.8–9). Merricat's hatred of the villagers is historic, preceding Constance's trial; as a child she imagines them 'sneaking and weaving and sidestepping servilely' (p.18) as they make their way along the highway and around the Blackwood's troublesome fences. In this atmosphere of antipathy and alienation Merricat retreats further and further from reality. While imagining that she could exist in another fantasy world, she can find no respite in either her family or the community from the antagonism that seems to surround her.

Adding to her outsider status, Merricat finds both protection and escape from an antagonistic world in the realm of magic. To everyone but Constance she seems witch-like, with her magic rituals that are an amalgam of folkloric practices and primitive magic, and her belief in omens and safeguards. When Merricat needs a solution she turns to magic; overwhelmed by Charles' oppressive presence Merricat 'lay back against the tree trunk and thought of magic' (p.71). One of Merricat's more bizarre routines is to go the attic every Thursday and wear 'their' clothes (p.41), hoping to gain power from her dead parents' garments. She asks Constance to bake a gingerbread man for her so she can call it Charles and eat it, thereby making the hated Charles disappear. She also takes great pleasure in creating a representation of Charles' head and burying it in a hole in the garden:

> The hole would hold his head nicely. I laughed when I found a round stone the right size, and scratched a face on it and buried it in the hole. 'Goodbye Charles,' I said. (p.89)

Merricat here is applying sympathetic magic, which is based on the idea that possessing the image of a person gives the witch or shaman some control over the destiny of that person. In using the gingerbread man named Charles and the round stone inscribed with his face, she is obliterating Charles, wishing him dead and gone.

Jackson positions Merricat as the author of the narrative that she controls. Merricat is, of course, the literal narrator of the text and as the protagonist she is also the instigator of many of the events of the text. In other ways Jackson indicates Merricat's power to shape events while remaining hidden, invisible to others, much like an author. Merricat watches as events unfurl, often on her little stool in the corner of the kitchen, or almost out of the frame of the action when visitors arrive. When Helen Clarke and Mrs Wright visit, Merricat almost disappears, while Constance takes their mother's place: 'She sat on the rose sofa with our mother's portrait looking down on her, while I sat in my small chair in the corner and watched' (p.24). Merricat even uses the language of fiction to describe the sisters' return to the house after the fire:

> I thought that we had somehow not found our way back correctly through the night, that we had somehow lost ourselves and come back through the wrong gap in time, or the wrong door, or the wrong fairy tale. (p.114)

Uncle Julian is convinced that Merricat doesn't exist; he never addresses her and neither does Merricat speak directly to him. But Merricat has prescience; like an author, she knows what will happen next and she determines how the plot will evolve. Finally, when Merricat is joined by Constance at the end of the novel, they both become observers and commentators, imbued with power by the villagers and invisible to them within their castle.

Constance Blackwood

Key quotes

'When I was small I thought Constance was a fairy princess … She was the most precious person in my world, always.' (pp.19–20)

'"I am so happy," Constance said at last, gasping. "Merricat, I am so happy." "I told you that you would like it on the moon."' (p.145)

Constance is Merricat's older sister and the two, along with Uncle Julian, make up the small remnant of the Blackwood family who live together in the house. Constance cooks and gardens, feeding the family and taking care of Uncle Julian. As her name suggests, Constance is a steadfast and loving presence in the lives of Merricat and Julian. Constance's character is important in the novel because she provides a counterpoint to Merricat's eccentricities and a stable base around which the surviving Blackwoods can gather. Constance's character does not change dramatically through the course of the novel, but she does gain insight, realising the trap that Charles was setting for her and eventually freeing herself from some of the constraints of meeting others' expectations.

Constance acts as a substitute mother to Merricat, providing love and care, making her food and, most importantly, offering her acceptance when the rest of the world is hostile to her. Similarly, Constance's kindness to Uncle Julian extends beyond providing him with meals and being a generous caregiver. She also gives him dignity and supports his wavering confidence with her own assurances:

> 'Constance?' Uncle Julian turned his wheel chair to face her. 'How was I?'
>
> 'Superb, Uncle Julian.' Constance stood up and went over to him and touched his old head lightly. 'You didn't need your notes at all.' (p.39)

The Blackwoods are a very staid and conservative family who 'rarely moved things; the Blackwoods were never much of a family for restlessness or stirring' (p.1). Their views on women were equally rigid, Uncle Julian commenting, 'our wives always did as they were told' (p.47). It is unusual, then, that Constance is cast in the role of housekeeper, cook and cleaner from a young age and that Mrs Blackwood, her mother, was permitted to relinquish this role. The reader is not given a reason for this, only Uncle Julian's reflection that he 'personally preferred to chance the arsenic' (p.36) than to eat Mrs Blackwood's cooking.

In all her actions Constance appears to be unselfish and effortlessly kind. She provides an almost saintly contrast – 'she was pink and white and golden, and nothing had ever seemed to dim the brightness of her' (p.20) – to Merricat's tomboyishness and reputation as 'a wicked, disobedient child' (p.34). Constance's virtuousness is further emphasised when she takes the blame and goes on trial for poisoning the family to spare Merricat. There are glimmers of Merricat's nature in Constance, however, since she does wash out the arsenic from the sugar bowl, not only destroying the evidence but suggesting that she may even have colluded with Merricat, since she knew that there was arsenic in the sugar.

The villagers seem convinced that Constance did murder the family, and they also suspect that both sisters are involved in the occult. While this suggestion is almost welcomed by Merricat, she wants Constance to embrace it with her. After neatening the house Merricat says that with their brooms they were 'like a pair of witches walking home' (p.69). Constance protests when Merricat says, 'Old witch ... you have a gingerbread house' (p.75), and Merricat observes as they trawl through their ruined kitchen that they were like 'two old ladies going through dead leaves looking for pennies' (p.120). While, during the novel, Constance dismisses Merricat's framing of themselves as witches, she changes at the resolution of the text, joking with Merricat about punishing a child: when Merricat says, 'I wonder if I *could* eat a child if I had the chance', Constance replies, 'I doubt if I could cook one' (p.146).

Change in Constance

When Charles arrives Constance begins to defer to him as the natural head of the house, accepting Charles' criticism of the way they live – 'I wonder how you stand it' (p.71). Constance seems to allow her autonomy and confidence to be eroded by Charles' criticisms. He persuades Constance that his way of seeing things is right and hers is wrong; Merricat says, 'now she frowned at me often, as though I somehow looked different to her' (p.78). Constance is so far in thrall to Charles that she regrets all her past kindnesses to Merricat and Uncle Julian, observing that Charles has made her 'realize how wrong I was' (p.79). The change that Charles inevitably brings is a change back to the patriarchal model. This model requires that women be subservient and accept their positions as domestic attendants, held in place by economic insecurity and uncertainty about their ability to govern themselves. 'That was her new way of thinking' (p.90), says Merricat, but she and Julian intervene by exposing Charles' anger and rigidity, and the house fire is the final step in sending him on his way.

Once Merricat and Constance reclaim possession of the house, albeit in a burnt and diminished state, Constance is once more able to take control of her domain. Despite Charles' disruption there is an immutable quality to Constance's genteel demeanour. She clears the rubble after the fire, retrieving what she can from the mess to make sure that life can be lived as she would like it: '"We will take our meals like ladies," she said, "using cups with handles"' (p.121).

Uncle Julian Blackwood

Key quotes

'"I have the newspaper clippings," Uncle Julian said uncertainly.' (p.32)

'He is dishonest. His father was dishonest. Both my brothers were dishonest … He is a bastard.' (p.83)

'You are a young bastard and I desire that you return to your father, who, to my shame, is my brother Arthur, and tell him I said so.' (p.92)

Uncle Julian is the brother of Merricat and Constance's father. He is important in the novel because he provides another view of the way the Blackwood family interacted when John Blackwood was head of the family. Julian's memory has been affected by the arsenic, but his dry sense of humour remains intact and he provides a great deal of the comedy of the novel. He takes delight in amusing his family and friends – 'Do you recall that I was very entertaining in the garden that morning, Constance?' (p.48) – and he maintains his dignity and sense of self-worth despite his sometimes addled mental state and Charles' attempts to undermine him.

Charles Blackwood

Key quotes

'"Cousin Mary doesn't like me," Charles said again to Jonas. "I wonder if Cousin Mary knows how I get even with people who don't like me?"' (p.70)

'"It's a crazy house," Charles said with conviction. "Constance, this is a crazy house."' (p.92)

'Charles looked at her and at me and at Uncle Julian. He was clearly baffled, unable to grasp his fingers tightly around anything he saw or heard; it was a joyful sight, to see the first twistings and turnings of the demon caught …' (p.94)

Charles is Merricat and Constance's cousin, and Julian's nephew. He arrives at the house saying that he wants to help the sisters, although his real intention is to take over John Blackwood's role as head of the house and control the Blackwood money. Charles is at once an agent of change and representative of stasis in the novel.

The change that Charles brings about is motivated by avarice; he insinuates himself into the Blackwood household with the intention of taking their money. To do that he realises he must first make Constance his domestic servant: '"She's too busy now," Charles said with his mouth full. "Your sister works like a slave"' (p.81). He then unseats Merricat and Julian from their positions in the family. He threatens Merricat directly: '"Come about a month from now, I wonder who *will* still be here? You," he said, "or me?"' (p.80).

Charles is also a representative of the status quo. He is not only the product of a deeply conservative family, but also represents the entrenched patriarchal structures that Merricat had escaped, but which persist in the outside world. Merricat follows him to the village, which has been extremely hostile to her, to see that he is part of the fabric there: 'when I saw him sit down on the benches with the other men I turned and went back to our house. If I went into the village shopping again Charles would be one of the men who watched me going past' (p.81).

When Charles flees the burning house and then returns to join the villagers who have gathered to watch the fire, his malice towards not only Merricat and Julian, but also Constance, becomes clear. Following the announcement of Julian's death, he calls from his position among the crowd, 'Did she kill him?' (p.109).

Minor characters

Jonas

Merricat's cat seems to be the only being besides Constance that Merricat really loves, and he follows her everywhere. Merricat is (or at least believes herself to be) able to understand him speaking.

Helen Clarke

Helen Clarke is an old friend of the Blackwood family, and one of the few people who hasn't abandoned them since the murders. She still comes to tea periodically, and she begins to urge Constance to rejoin society.

Stella

Stella runs a cafe in the village where Merricat always stops on her way home from doing the shopping. Merricat goes there not because she wants to, but because she feels the need to show that she is not afraid of the villagers.

Jim Donell

One of the villagers, Jim particularly hates the Blackwoods and represents the worst of the villagers' attitudes towards them. He is also the chief firefighter, and although he leads the effort to put out the fire he is also a ringleader of the mob.

Jim Clarke

Jim Clarke is Helen Clarke's husband. She brings him to the Blackwood house after it burns to try to get Merricat and Constance to come and live in the Clarkes' house.

Mrs Lucille Wright

Mrs Wright is friends with Helen Clarke and accompanies her to tea at the Blackwoods' house near the beginning of the novel. Mrs Wright's curiosity about the poisoning and the trial gives Uncle Julian an audience, while making Helen Clarke deeply uncomfortable.

Joe Dunham

One of the hostile villagers, Joe Dunham comes into Stella's cafe and joins in Jim Donell's harassment of Merricat. He feels bitter because he once fixed the Blackwoods' broken step and never received payment for his work. In truth, Constance refused to pay him because he did a bad job.

Dr Levy

Uncle Julian's doctor seems uneasy around Merricat but is kind to Uncle Julian. He finds Julian dead after the fire. Later, he returns with Jim Clarke to try to make sure the sisters are all right.

Mr Elbert

The owner of the grocery store where Merricat goes, Mr Elbert tries to get her out the door as quickly as possible.

Mr Harler

While the villagers ruin the house, Mr Harler – a junk dealer – makes a pile of the junk that they throw outside.

THEMES, IDEAS & VALUES

Family

Key quotes

'The Blackwoods had always lived in our house, and kept their things in order …' (p.1)

'The people of the village have always hated us.' (p.4)

The term 'family' in the 1950s and early 1960s, when *We Have Always Lived in the Castle* was written, commonly referred to a nuclear family consisting of a father, a mother and two or three children living in the same house. The Blackwoods add another dimension to that definition because they also have the impoverished Uncle Julian and his wife, Dorothy, living with them. After the deaths of the rest of the family, only a stub of the original family lives on in the Blackwood house, the members of which make up a reduced family of their own. Although Merricat, Constance and Uncle Julian manage to redefine 'family' so that they themselves are content, their arrangements are disapproved of by the villagers who wish them gone – Jim Donell says sarcastically, 'Anyone would think … that they wasn't wanted' (p.13) – and by their own extended family, who leave Merricat in an orphanage during her sister's trial rather than be associated with the scandal.

In a traditional family the head of the household, at the apex of the hierarchy, is the father, who controls the money and determines who has what power in the family unit. In a patrilineal family the father passes on property and power to the male heirs. The Blackwood family was both patriarchal and patrilineal, with each generation of male descendants inheriting the house, property and wealth of the preceding Blackwood patriarch. The son, Thomas Blackwood, who would have inherited the estate instead of Constance or Merricat, was also poisoned at the family dinner and so the sisters occupy the house by default in the absence of any male claim to the inheritance.

Until Charles intrudes, the sisters and Uncle Julian live harmoniously, if eccentrically, in their unconventional family unit. Constance dresses prettily and is a template for the perfect mother, caring for Uncle Julian and Merricat and cooking all the meals; Uncle Julian's physical and mental deterioration precludes him from taking on the role of patriarch and he is content to be occupied with his 'papers'; Merricat might be seen as the fanciful controller of the group, except that Uncle Julian doesn't acknowledge her existence and Constance dismisses her outbursts with 'Silly Merricat' (e.g. p.45, p.51, p.59). Each individual seems to chart their own course and live contentedly in their own construction of the family unit.

Through this eccentric group Jackson suggests to the reader that family can be constructed not only according to predetermined social conventions but also through an intention to live harmoniously as a collective. When Cousin Charles arrives, he exerts himself to re-establish the 'normal' hierarchical family order, with himself as the surrogate father, Constance as wife and mother, and Julian and Merricat as errant children. Charles is a 'demon and a ghost' (p.83), as Merricat calls him, because he is bringing back to life the patriarchal structure which Merricat and, to a certain extent, Constance, had so violently overturned. Charles, a member of the Blackwoods' extended family, represents the 'ghost' or haunting spirit of the patriarchy that they had banished.

In the final chapter of the novel, Merricat and Constance seem to transcend the idea of a family unit and become instead narrators of the life that they observe from their position behind the shuttered windows and the locked front door of their castle. They have won power through their persistence in shutting themselves off from society and its definition of family, becoming, as a result, enigmatic survivors. At the end of the novel they are at once feared and immortalised by the villagers who bring them offerings to propitiate (appease) them.

Outsiders

Key quotes

'I was afraid that they might touch me and the mothers would come at me like a flock of taloned hawks …' (p.7)

'She wouldn't behave like this anywhere else, I thought, only here.' (Merricat of Helen Clarke, p.29)

Normality, on the surface, might seem to be a good thing, but in *We Have Always Lived in the Castle* the representatives of 'normal' society are mostly frightening, avaricious and vengeful. Those who embody conformity are united outside the boundaries of the Blackwood house, while the inhabitants of the house become reclusive, guarding themselves from the antipathy of the rest of the world.

In this novel Jackson explores what it means to be excluded from the community one lives in, and how exclusion can lead to hatred and depersonalisation of those rejected. Merricat, Constance and Julian are jeered at and mocked by the villagers, and a children's sing-song taunt is chanted at Merricat and Constance if they appear in public:

> Merricat, said Connie, would you like a cup of tea?
> Oh no, said Merricat, you'll poison me.
> Merricat, said Connie, would you like to go to sleep?
> Down in the boneyard ten feet deep! (p.16)

As the remaining Blackwood family members become further ostracised, they are increasingly made into the repositories for the villagers' woes. In Stella's cafe Donell 'picks on' Merricat while his friend, Dunham, blames the Blackwoods for his own faulty workmanship:

> 'Me,' Dunham said, 'I can always tell people I fixed their broken step once and never got paid for it.' That was true. Constance had sent me out to tell him that we wouldn't pay the carpenter's prices for a raw board nailed crookedly across the step when what he was supposed to do was build it trim and new. (p.14)

The Blackwood sisters are victimised by the community that they should be a part of, and harassed by villagers who do not understand them: 'They had picnics on the lawn and took pictures of each other standing in front of the house and let their dogs run in the garden. They wrote their names on the walls and on the front door' (p.57).

This is not to suggest that the antagonism between villagers and landowners goes only one way. The Blackwoods pride themselves on being superior to the villagers, with their 'dirty little houses' (p.4). The idea of a class divide between the Blackwoods and the villagers is clearly outlined in Merricat's caustic observation:

> All of the village was of a piece, a time, and a style; it was as though the people needed the ugliness of the village, and fed on it ... The blight on the village never came from the Blackwoods; the villagers belonged here and the village was the only proper place for them. (p.6)

This class conflict is exacerbated by the murders that happen in the Blackwood house, giving the villagers more fodder to gossip about their gentrified neighbours, and this gossip turns to exclusion as their positions become entrenched. The distance between the villagers and the Blackwood family becomes further embedded as the murders at the Blackwood house are made public through Constance's trial.

Merricat, Constance and, to an extent, Uncle Julian reject the society that surrounds them, making their own household rules and abiding by their own guidelines. They only barely tolerate occasional incursions from Helen Clarke and the Carringtons, friends of the Blackwood parents, but their solitary lives have become embedded habit; they are not welcome in the outside world, and they do not welcome strangers.

Eventually, after the catastrophic events of the fire, the death of Uncle Julian and the banishment of Charles, the sisters reject society in its entirety. Their lives confined to the kitchen and the cellar, they find a kind of happiness that is the opposite of that encapsulated in the American Dream. Far from the notion held by Charles and the villagers that they revelled in their money – 'I knew they talked about the money hidden in our house, as though it were great heaps of golden coins' (p.7) – the sisters finally live without any use for money at all, never going to the village again to shop but subsisting on the food offerings from the frightened villagers or what they have stored in the pantry or growing in the kitchen garden.

When the villagers bring food to the house for the sisters to eat, it is not because they feel they must be kind to the Blackwoods to make reparation for the damage they have caused, despite the apologies that accompany the gifts. Rather, the food is a kind of offering to appease the sisters. As outsiders who survive complete rejection by society, Merricat and Constance become objects of fear.

Jackson has written often about the fearsome violence of the mob, most notably in her short story 'The Lottery', which centres on a town in which an annual lottery is held, the 'winner' of which faces an unpleasant fate. In both texts the mob directs its murderous intent towards outsiders, people already marginalised and isolated by society, and these victims of violence are further demonised by the crowd once they find that they have some power over them. The sisters, outsiders who have been attacked, vilified and scorned, finally achieve an almost mythical status where they live. The more that the Blackwood sisters are proved to be 'the other' by society, the more their power as an unknown and, perhaps, avenging force grows.

Domesticity and female roles

Key quotes

'In this village the men stayed young and did the gossiping and the women aged with grey evil weariness and stood silently waiting for the men to get up and come home.' (p.3)

'… the deeply colored rows of jellies and pickles and bottled vegetables and fruit … stood side by side in our cellar and would stand there forever, a poem by the Blackwood women.' (p.42)

The setting of the novel is consciously limited, focusing on the Blackwood house and grounds, and the narrow confines of the path that Merricat takes through the village when she does the shopping. Within this narrow but detailed setting Jackson plays out the power dynamic that is at work between men and women, both in the house and in the village. The village women are indoors, at home, while the men occupy the external spaces at their leisure. Even when it comes to making offerings of food to the Blackwood sisters, 'the men came home from work and the women had the baskets ready for them to carry over' (p.139).

The same rule applies for the Blackwood men and women; the women stay in the house and the men occupy the outer world. Merricat does not fit the mould of the other women, however. She is not a domestic young woman, although she does help Constance with some housework; Merricat is a creature of the outdoors, happiest when building shelters, hiding in the grass, burying treasure and creating safeguards to protect herself and Constance from the rest of the world.

She spends most of her time outdoors, and when she does come back to the house she comes 'trailing mist from the creek' (p.59). When the house and the sisters' clothes are burned, she suggests she wears 'a suit of leaves. At once. With acorns for buttons … a lining of moss, for cold winter days, and a hat made of bird feathers' (p.135). Her safest hiding spot, and a welcome alternative to the house, is in a hidden shelter that she constructs by the creek.

Constance, on the other hand, is the consummate housekeeper. She is tied to her cooking and gardening routines and seems to enjoy her role as Uncle Julian and Merricat's protector. Constance's kitchen is immaculate and her devotion to growing and preserving food is a preoccupation handed down from generation to generation of Blackwood women.

Constance and Merricat maintain the Blackwood house meticulously in their systematic neatening routine. The sisters keep their father's bedroom and study exactly as it was when he died, and their mother's drawing room, an altar to her, is kept 'shining and silky' (p.24). While the masculine exterior of the house is 'stern, unwelcoming' (p.20), its interior is both richly furnished and replete with china, sets of silverware, preserves and dinner sets, the accumulated dowries of generations of Blackwood women. The interior of the house represents the domain of the wives and daughters of the Blackwood family, their physical contributions and domestic work making up the comfort of the household. Merricat and Constance, after the death of most of the family, tend the interior of the house as carefully as if it were a shrine, while the exterior is left wild, inhabited only by Merricat and Jonas.

The house

Key quote

> 'Almost all of our life was lived toward the back of the house, on the lawn and the garden where no one else ever came.' (p.20)

The last three novels that Jackson wrote, *The Sundial* (1958), *The Haunting of Hill House* (1959) and *We Have Always Lived in the Castle* (1962), are often called her 'house' novels, because they focus on the ways that families live in their houses, and the way each shapes the other.

The title of the novel, *We Have Always Lived in the Castle,* points to the significance of the house in the text. It is an image from a fairytale, an improbable 'castle' in New Hampshire. Externally, it is a monument to the Blackwood lineage; internally, it is a shrine to the women who have created the domestic inheritance. The house is anthropomorphised, reacting and responding to its inhabitants. Constance takes the burning of the house as a personal affront: '"We neatened it just the other day," she said. "It has no *right* to burn"' (p.102). Its exterior is seen as forbidding by strangers at the beginning of the novel and at the end it is seen as 'a tomb' by sightseers (p.140). However, it is a haven for Merricat and Constance. But while the house can protect its inhabitants, it also harbours the secrets of past generations, represented to the reader through Uncle Julian's discarded wheelchair and the locked rooms. Merricat says, at the novel's conclusion, 'We learned, from listening, that all the strangers could see from outside ... was a great ruined structure overgrown with vines, barely recognizable as a house' (p.146).

Eventually, Merricat replaces her life outdoors with her existence with Constance in the invulnerable house – the 'castle' of the novel's title. Merricat's 'little house ... on the moon' (p.14) is replaced by another idyllic fantasy, a castle in which she and Constance can live. There are, of course, advantages to living in a fairytale castle. Merricat promises Constance that she will 'go on my winged horse and bring you cinnamon and thyme, emeralds and clove, cloth of gold and cabbages' (p.133), but the castle that the sisters create also has connotations of a myth, like an isolated, folkloric castle created out of sequestration (exile), with connotations of Rapunzel, the princess in the tower, and many more folk tales of female imprisonment.

The fire

Key quote

'Although I did not perceive it then, time and the orderly pattern of our old days had ended ...' (p.116)

Jackson anthropomorphises both the house and the fire that destroys it, making the house a castle and the fire into an important symbol of catharsis in Chapter Nine. The house should 'remember' Constance when she returns to it in its ruined state, 'the kitchen door ... ought surely to recognize the touch of her hand'. The house also 'seemed to shiver when she opened the door' (p.113). Meanwhile, the fire, consuming the house as if it were human, 'had had to be content with the bedrooms and the attic' (p.113). When ash from Charles' pipe burns a hole in the brocade in the drawing room, Merricat does not tell Constance because she 'hoped that the house, injured, would reject him by itself' (p.78).

The fire is catastrophic, but it is also an important symbol of cleansing; while painfully destroying their only habitable and safe place to live, the fire has also removed the weight of the generations of Blackwoods that have forced the young women into the service of their memory. The fire has taken away all the altars to the preceding generations, such as the father's study where the wealth of the Blackwoods was kept in the safe, the family dining room where the paterfamilias sat at the head of the table, and their mother's drawing room, which is presided over by a painting of their mother and had to be assiduously maintained in her memory, even though, during her lifetime, the sisters 'had never been allowed in here' (p.24).

Catharsis is traditionally understood as a purification process in which an individual's or a community's guilt is purged so that they can begin to live their lives anew. Fire is often the medium for catharsis in mythology, folklore and even in nature, when a forest fire burns off old growth and allows new shoots to come through. The fire relieves Constance and Merricat of the burden of the past and also helps them to resolve the conflict that plagues their lives – they no longer need to give even token acknowledgement to the patriarchal family and community that they live in. Merricat celebrates the new life the fire has afforded them, reflecting at the end of the novel:

> I thought that perhaps my six blue marbles had been buried to protect a house which no longer existed and had no connection with the house where we lived now, and where we were very happy. (p.145)

Folklore, magic and nature

Key quotes

'All the omens spoke of change.' (p.40)

'On Sunday mornings I examined my safeguards … so long as they were where I had put them nothing could get in to harm us.' (p.41)

Jackson had some expertise in witchcraft, writing *The Witchcraft of Salem Village*, a nonfiction book, in 1956. Her personal library also included many books on folklore, magic and witchcraft. Her husband, Stanley Hyman, ran a very popular course at Bennington College on myth, ritual and literature. This rich knowledge of fairytales, myths, magic and witchcraft informs much of *We Have Always Lived in the Castle*, particularly the characterisation of Merricat.

Merricat's reliance on magic as a way of protecting herself from a threatening outside world is manifested in her many 'safeguards': the book nailed to a tree; the marbles in the creek; her buried baby teeth; the silver dollars left in a box under a broken step and, finally, Uncle Julian's wheelchair. All these totemic objects criss-crossing the land around the house play an important part, in Merricat's thinking, in creating 'a powerful taut web which never loosened, but held fast to guard us' (p.41). She also uses 'magic' and nature to expel Charles from the house. Believing Charles to be a ghost or a demon, she tries to confuse him by breaking mirrors, littering his room and changing the position of objects so that he will be disoriented and 'would not be able to find books or clothes and would be lost in a room of leaves and broken sticks' (p.87).

The 'magic' that Merricat uses is incapable of protecting the sisters, but the idea of a magic solution is a calming antidote to the hostile world in which she is powerless. Merricat is an intelligent young woman who is also quick-witted and capable of reading character accurately. She knows that Charles is acting out of malice and self-interest in trying to unseat Uncle Julian and Merricat from their home and keep Constance as his domestic slave, because she reads the signs of ill-intent in Charles' unconscious behaviour.

Merricat sees Charles as a ghost because, in a sense, he is one, bringing back the spectre of the patriarchy into a household of people who have not long since unchained themselves from it. The smoke from Charles' pipe fills the air, metaphorically staking a claim on the house, and he even, unknowingly, burns a hole in the pink upholstery of her mother's drawing room with his matches, polluting the altar to their mother that the sisters kept 'shining and silky' (p.24).

Even Merricat's most bizarre behaviour is understandable if we consider that both her instincts and her reading have drawn her into the natural world because it provides a safe haven and a source of solace. Jackson often uses oppositions and mirroring in her writing. That is, she uses images or characters who are the opposite of another image or character, or who mirror or reflect similar properties of the image or character. For example, Jackson sets the villagers and the gentry in opposition to represent class conflict in the novel, while Charles mirrors John Blackwood in both looks and disposition. In the case of Merricat's attraction to the natural world, Jackson uses oppositions to juxtapose the brutal demands of household and village with the sanctuary of nature.

At the height of the dramatic action in the novel, with the house burnt and the villagers working themselves up into such a pitch of murderous fury that one villager suggests that they 'put them back in the house and start the fire all over again' (p.108), Merricat drags Constance to the safety of the woods. Here, as always, Merricat finds sanctuary from the hostile world of the village in its opposite, the natural world:

> When I felt my feet leave the grass of the lawn and touch the soft mossy ground of the path through the woods and knew that the trees had closed in around us I stopped and put my arms around Constance. 'It's all over,' I told her, and held her tight. 'It's all right,' I said, 'all right now.' (p.110)

References to Merricat's connection to the natural world abound throughout the novel. She regularly runs away from the house to the woods to find peace and security, even creating a shelter out of branches and leaves where she can stay during the night. Surprisingly, Constance sees this as part of Merricat's nature and does not seem to worry about her long absences, saying 'Silly Merricat' rather than scolding her. When she returns from the woods to the house she is 'trailing mist from the creek' (p.59) and her preferred costume when everything is destroyed is that of the Green Man, a suit made of leaves and acorns.

Ironically, at the resolution of the novel, despite knowing that nature provides a shield for her and is therefore part of her magical protection, Merricat must forgo her trips outdoors, which she does for the sake of her sister. She confines herself to the ruined house and does not venture beyond it because of the trauma caused to Constance; Merricat finally stays housebound with her sister because the creek 'was much too far from Constance' (p.140).

Feminism

Key quotes

'... our mother had been born there and by rights it should have belonged to Constance.' (p.3)

'I thought that tomorrow he would be wearing our father's signet ring, and I wondered if he would make Constance put on our mother's pearls.' (p.80)

Jackson is often referred to as a protofeminist; that is, she wrote about feminist issues before feminism was a concept in wide circulation. Writing in the 1950s and early 1960s, she critiqued the domestic roles that women were allocated by society at that time and the psychological toll that being a homemaker took on the women of that period. It is easy to forget that as late as the early 1970s, US President Nixon lauded the American Dream that involved a husband being the affluent breadwinner while his wife was the attractive homemaker.

There are only four main characters in *We Have Always Lived in the Castle,* and each one tells us something about the roles of women in society. Merricat, of course, violently rejects patriarchal control. Constance is the epitome of the female 'attractive homemaker', characterised by Merricat as 'pink and white and golden ... nothing had ever seemed to dim the brightness of her' (p.20). From a young age she has also been responsible for cooking and cleaning the house, something she seems to enjoy and excel at. Constance, despite being depicted as a 'fairy princess' (p.19), does passively join Merricat in overturning the patriarchal order among the Blackwoods when they are poisoned: she delays calling the doctor until the poison has taken effect and it is too late; she washes out the sugar bowl that contained the arsenic; she says that the family deserved to die.

Charles is represented as a 'ghost' (p.83) of the patriarchal Blackwood line as he tries to re-establish the male hierarchical order in the house. He assumes John Blackwood's place at the head of the table, undermines Constance's confidence in her decision-making and threatens Uncle Julian and Merricat with expulsion from the house if they don't bend to his authority.

Uncle Julian plays a small role in developing the idea of female power in the novel since he is part of the patriarchal order but he acts more as a witness to the way the Blackwood men, including Charles, behave.

DIFFERENT INTERPRETATIONS

Different interpretations arise from different responses to a text. Over time, a text will evoke a wide range of responses from its readers, who may come from various social or cultural groups and live in very different places and historical periods. Responses by critics and reviewers can be published in newspapers, journals and books, both online and in print. They can also be expressed in discussions among readers in the media, classrooms, book groups and so on.

While there is no single correct reading or interpretation of a text, it is important to understand that an interpretation is more than a personal opinion – it is the justification of a point of view on the text. To present an interpretation of a text based on your point of view, you must use a logical argument and support it with relevant evidence from the text.

Critical viewpoints

Since its publication in 1962 *We Have Always Lived in the Castle* has attracted a wide variety of critical viewpoints. In the 1960s the novel was seen as a horror and a mystery story. Popularly, it was also viewed as a mystery novel without a detective to solve the mystery. *The New Yorker* ran a cartoon depicting two women in mink coats saying that the book is about someone putting arsenic in the sugar bowl and they don't know who did it. Critics rated the book highly, however, because of Jackson's adept writing, the purposeful ambiguity and the novel's suspenseful tone.

In 1967 Stuart Woodruff wrote that 'the moral of Miss Jackson's persuasive fable … is to make us feel the moral superiority of "life on the moon" to a drab and mean existence in the village'. He saw the novel as representing a conflict between two worlds and two value systems (Woodruff 1967).

By the 1980s, with the focus on the women's movement and following the publication of influential books such as *The Second Sex* (Simone de Beauvoir), *The Female Eunuch* (Germaine Greer) and *The Feminine Mystique* (Betty Friedan), the focus in criticism turned to sexual politics and Jackson's text began to be read not as a horror or mystery but as a novel about the overthrow of the patriarchy. Lynette Carpenter writes that a self-contained community of women, however small, is preferable, in Jackson's view, to a hostile, patriarchal world (Carpenter 1984).

Psychological interpretations base their readings of the text on Freudian and post-Freudian psychological theories. In fact, texts have been interpreted through a psychological lens since long before Freud. In ancient Greece, Aristotle wrote about catharsis in theatre, positing that this was the pivotal moment in a tragedy when both the protagonist and the audience were 'cleansed' of their guilt as a result of a revelation or destruction. Later psychological theorists, influenced by Freud, Jung and Lacan, explain that there is more meaning in the text than the available literal meaning of the words used by the author.

Jackson's work is very accessible via a psychological critique as she employs an unreliable narrator, Merricat, to relate the family tragedy of the Blackwoods. Merricat's relationship with her mother, a major focus in psychological interpretations, is left naggingly absent in *We Have Always Lived in the Castle*. By contrast, we know many details about John Blackwood, who is 'a man very fond of his person … Given to adorning himself, and not overly clean' (p.78), and who holds debts and 'favours' as accountable objects in his wealth. The mother is left as an important yet absent figure; her memory is enshrined in the drawing room, with its costly drapes and furnishings, and the prominent portrait of her that oversees her domain. A psychological criticism would pay close attention to the missing mother. It would also be interested in the notion of the divided self. Gilbert and Gubar (1979) suggest that female authors depict female characters as repressing their independence and individuality in a patriarchal society and, as a result, becoming 'the madwoman in the attic', like Bertha Rochester in *Jane Eyre*. Perceptive readers will notice that Jackson makes a reference to the maddened Bertha, imprisoned in the attic of her matrimonial home, in the naming of Mrs Blackwood's house the Rochester house.

These are the major themes explored by critics, but there are many other ways of reading the text that co-exist with these approaches. Critics have used biographical detail to explain the character of Merricat (who is based on one of Jackson's daughters). Some have also suggested that Jackson drew on her own experiences with depression and agoraphobia in her depiction of Merricat's mental state. Other critics explore the themes of the text through the references to food throughout, often connecting this motif to the roles of women in the 1950s.

Two interpretations

Interpretation 1: *We Have Always Lived in the Castle* explores the difficulty of being an outsider.

Merricat, Constance and Uncle Julian are ostracised by the society in which they live, making their world increasingly constricted; ironically, the further they withdraw into themselves the greater the suspicion and hostility directed at them. Shirley Jackson, in *We Have Always Lived in the Castle*, explores the debilitating effects of being labelled as 'other'. Being 'the other' not only diminishes the outsiders themselves, but also causes them to shrink from further exposure to the groups who suppress them.

The Blackwoods were always conscious that the villagers resented their wealth, but once Constance is tried for poisoning her family the strained relationship between the villagers and the Blackwoods becomes one of frank hostility; the family are certainly outsiders to the villagers. Merricat makes restricted trips into the unfriendly village for food and books, but these trips are fraught with menace and she feels 'vulnerable and exposed' (p.5) to the ill-will of the villagers. After suffering the stares and gossiping of the women while shopping Merricat forces herself, 'out of pride' (p.11), to go into Stella's cafe, where she is harassed and bullied by the men. The children follow her out of the village, calling:

> Merricat, said Connie, would you like a cup of tea?
> Oh no, said Merricat, you'll poison me. (p.16)

This chant fixes the idea of Constance as a murderer and Merricat as an object of ridicule.

Merricat, Constance and Uncle Julian live a sequestered existence in their house, away from the insults of the villagers, where they manage their lives and their fear of the outside world through strict routines. Merricat buries a series of magical safeguards that form 'a powerful taut web which never loosened, but held fast to guard us' (p.41) from the evil of the world, and Constance never ventures further than the garden, to avoid the jeers of the villagers.

By using Merricat as the narrator, Jackson positions the reader to sympathise with the outsiders and the unusual and elaborate precautions the Blackwood sisters take to avoid being harassed. Their routines, Merricat's 'magic' and Uncle Julian's ramblings make sense when we see, from Merricat's point of view, the malice of the villagers and the cruelty of her upbringing. As outsiders, the remaining Blackwood family of two women and a wheelchair-bound uncle must endure as a unit, despite the difficulties of making themselves self-sufficient.

As a young girl Merricat was an outsider who was 'always in disgrace' and 'a wicked, disobedient child' (p.34), and this independent spirit led to her parents punishing her with the withdrawal of food and affection. Merricat's response to this exclusion is to create a fantasy world in which she is able to escape on a winged horse to live 'on the moon' (p.44). Her final act of rebellion is to poison everyone in the family, except for Constance, whom she loves. Merricat is not the only outsider in her family; Constance, too, as a child had to step into an adult role and take over the cooking and housekeeping, while Thomas, their brother and heir to the Blackwood fortune, 'who possessed many of his father's more forceful traits of character' (p.34), was indulged and allowed to be active, doing all the things that Merricat was punished for doing.

On a broader scale Jackson questions the way that women are precluded from entering fully into society. Women are outsiders in a male-dominated world and their lives are made challenging because of their lack of agency. The women in the village live an indoor existence with occasional excursions to the grocery store for shopping, while the men sit together outside and gossip until they return home for a meal. However, even from this position of oppression, the village women unite with the men against the more obvious outsiders to punish them.

Once the pent-up hatred of the villagers for the surviving Blackwoods is released by the fire at the house, the real damage caused by ostracising outsiders is revealed. The villagers become a mob, smashing the windows and contents of the house, surrounding the frightened young women and threatening, 'Put them back in the house and start the fire all over again' (p.108). The community, dehumanised by their exclusion of people who are not like themselves and empowered by their sense of now having the upper hand, set upon the young women, their wild behaviour making Merricat fearful that 'they were going to join hands and dance around us, singing' (p.108).

Jackson makes the point that, denied a sense of purpose and with no power to fight the structure that excludes them, individuals become alienated and have a diminished sense of self. The villagers, by violently rejecting Merricat and Constance as outsiders, cause immense damage not only to the individuals they ostracise but to their own humanity.

Interpretation 2: Sometimes being an outsider is the only way to survive.

Being an outsider and bearing the burden of one's 'otherness' can be preferable to being locked into a powerless position and losing one's selfhood, both within one's family and in society. To different degrees, Merricat, Constance and Uncle Julian come to accept their roles as outsiders and manage to go on, by finding humour in their predicament and solace in routine or distraction. Despite the losses experienced by Merricat and Constance, eventually they are able to survive, though only when they live entirely apart from society in their ruined house.

Clearly considered outcasts by the villagers, Merricat, Constance and Uncle Julian are also relegated to the role of outsiders by their previous friends, who make sporadic and tentative attempts to see them and who still keep a watchful eye on their oddness even when visiting for tea. When Helen Clarke visits, bringing with her a reluctant but morbidly curious witness in 'frightened' Mrs Wright (p.25), the Blackwoods endure the woman's voyeuristic interest by deflecting her questions using black humour. When she enquires into the details of the poisoning, Uncle Julian undercuts the seriousness of the crime with mordant humour, a protective technique used by all three Blackwoods. Mrs Wright strongly interjects that Constance 'should not have been doing the cooking' (p.35) and Julian counters with dark humour that if they knew she was going to poison them, 'we would have been blindly unselfish to encourage her to cook under such circumstances' (p.36). Further, when Merricat is under threat of being expelled by Charles from her own house, she manages to wring some grim humour from his angry outburst:

> 'We are going to have a long talk after dinner,' Charles said.
> '*Solanum dulcamara*,' I told him.
> 'What?' he said.
> 'Deadly nightshade,' Constance said. (p.100)

Jackson creates a wider setting for the study of outsiders by examining the status of women as outsiders in *We Have Always Lived in the Castle*. In both in the Blackwood family and in the village, their actions are limited by strict gender roles; they are forced, just as Merricat and Constance are, into compliance with a rigid set of norms that confine women to indoor, domestic tasks while men interact with the external world at their pleasure. Lacking distraction and humour, the women in the village 'aged with grey evil weariness and stood silently waiting for the men to get up and come home' (p.3). This lowly status and lack of agency are the very things that Merricat rebels against, and the reason why Merricat and Constance prefer to accept their positions as outsiders.

Merricat may not have had to make a transition from insider to outsider, as she always seems to have been an outsider to everyone in her family except Constance. She was 'always in disgrace' (p.34), constantly punished for her behaviour by having food and love withdrawn. But she embraces the role of outsider in preference to being dominated and diminished. Despite the constant rebukes from her family, she continues to rebel against them and the power they hold over her, culminating in the final murderous act that frees her of the constraints of her family but cements her position as an outsider in society.

Constance, on the other hand, is mostly compliant in taking on the role of housekeeper for the Blackwood family and she feels the strain of being an outsider more. Early in the novel she is already contemplating a return to society, telling Merricat, 'sooner or later I will have to take a first step' (p.24). Constance willingly accepts Charles' appearance at the house and, albeit hesitantly at first, complies with his attempts to take on the role of patriarch. Under Charles' influence she blames herself for the family's isolation, saying, 'We should have faced the world and tried to live normal lives ... We should have been living like other people' (p.82), despite the fact that it was 'other people' who rejected them.

Finally, after the villagers destroy their house, Merricat and Constance do find some peace in isolation. The position of outsider is not such a burden to Merricat, but eventually Constance, too, sees that isolation is the only key to survival in a hostile world.

QUESTIONS & ANSWERS

This section focuses on your own analytical writing on the text, and gives you strategies for producing high-quality responses in your coursework and exam essays.

Essay writing – an overview

An essay on a literary work is a formal and serious piece of writing that presents your point of view on the text, usually in response to a given topic. Your 'point of view' in an essay is your interpretation of the meaning of the text's language, structure, characters, situations and events, supported by detailed analysis of textual evidence.

Analyse – don't summarise

In your essays it is important to avoid simply summarising what happens in a text.

- A **summary** is a description or paraphrase (retelling in different words) of the characters and events. For example: 'Macbeth has a horrifying vision of a dagger dripping with blood before he goes to murder King Duncan.'
- An **analysis** is an explanation of the real meaning or significance that lies 'beneath' the text's words (and images, for a film). For example: 'Macbeth's vision of a bloody dagger shows how deeply uneasy he is about the violent act he is contemplating, and conveys his sense that supernatural forces are impelling him to act.'

A limited amount of summary is sometimes necessary to let your reader know which part of the text you wish to discuss. However, always keep this to a minimum and follow it immediately with your analysis of what this part of the text is really telling us.

Plan your essay

Carefully plan your essay so that you have a clear idea of what you are going to say. The plan ensures that your ideas flow logically, that your argument remains consistent and that you stay on the topic. An essay plan should be a list of **brief dot points** covering no more than half a page.

- Include your central argument or main contention – a concise statement of your overall response to the topic.
- Write three or four dot points for each paragraph, indicating the main idea and evidence/examples from the text. Note that in your essay you will need to *expand* on these points and *analyse* the evidence.

Structure your essay

An essay is a complete, self-contained piece of writing. It has a clear beginning (the introduction), middle (several body paragraphs) and end (the last paragraph or conclusion). It must also have a central argument that runs throughout, linking each paragraph to form a coherent whole. See examples of introductions and conclusions in the 'Analysing a sample topic' and 'Sample answer' sections.

The introduction establishes your overall response to the topic. It includes your main contention and outlines the main evidence you will refer to in the course of the essay. Write your introduction *after* you have done a plan and *before* you write the rest of the essay.

The body paragraphs argue your case – they present evidence from the text and explain how this evidence supports your argument. Each body paragraph needs:

- a strong **topic sentence** (usually the first sentence) that states the main point being made in the paragraph
- **evidence** from the text, including some brief quotations
- **analysis** of the textual evidence, with **explanation** of its significance and how it supports your argument
- **links back to the topic** in one or more statements, usually towards the end of the paragraph.

Connect the body paragraphs so that your discussion flows smoothly. Use some linking words and phrases such as 'similarly' and 'on the other hand', though don't start every paragraph like this. Another strategy is to use a significant word from the last sentence of one paragraph in the first sentence of the next.

Use key terms from the topic – or synonyms for them – throughout, so the relevance of your discussion to the topic is always clear.

The conclusion ties everything together and finishes the essay. It includes strong statements that emphasise your central argument and provide a clear response to the topic.

Avoid simply restating the points made earlier in the essay – this will end on a very flat note and imply that you have run out of ideas and vocabulary. The conclusion should be a logical extension of what you have written, not just a repetition or summary of it. Writing an effective conclusion can be a challenge. Try using these tips:

- Start by linking back to the final sentence of the second-last paragraph, rather than leaping to your main contention straight away – this helps your writing to flow.
- Use synonyms and expressions with equivalent meanings to vary your vocabulary. This allows you to reinforce your line of argument without being repetitive.
- When planning your essay, think of one or two broad statements or observations about the text's wider meaning. These should be related to the topic and your overall argument. Keep them for the conclusion, since they will give you something 'new' to say but still follow logically from your discussion. The introduction will be focused on the topic, but the conclusion can present a wider view of the text.

Essay topics

1. 'Family is the cause of all the problems in *We Have Always Lived in the Castle*.' Do you agree?
2. 'Merricat and Constance finally find safety in their ruined house, but they sacrifice their freedom.' Discuss.
3. 'In *We Have Always Lived in the Castle* the women are stronger than the men.' Discuss.
4. 'In *We Have Always Lived in the Castle* the villagers are motivated by fear more than anything else.' Do you agree?
5. "The world is full of terrible people," says Merricat. How accurate is Merricat's assessment of the people around her?
6. 'In *We Have Always Lived in the Castle* the Blackwoods see change as a threat.' Do you agree?
7. 'Safety is ultimately restored for the Blackwood sisters, but at what cost?' Discuss.
8. 'Merricat and Constance are both the heroes and the villains in *We Have Always Lived in the Castle*.' Discuss.
9. 'The choices Merricat makes are always based on self-preservation.' Do you agree?
10. How does Jackson create an atmosphere of menace in *We Have Always Lived in the Castle?*

Vocabulary for writing on *We Have Always Lived in the Castle*

Anthropomorphism: Speaking or writing about an inanimate object, such as a house, as if it were human.

Foreshadowing: Giving the reader a hint or a preview of what is to follow.

Gothic: A literary genre that features an atmosphere of gloom and terror; a Gothic text often includes supernatural events and a large, haunted house, and explores the notion of the past inhabiting the present.

Irony: A literary device in which a deeper, usually contradictory, meaning lies beneath the surface meaning of words.

Magical thinking: The idea that an individual can influence events by using words, thoughts or objects unrelated to those events. For example, Merricat nails her father's notebook to a tree in order to keep out strangers.

Mirroring: Using an image or a character to reflect another image or character. For example, Charles Blackwood reflects the patriarchal role of John Blackwood; he looks like the deceased father, sits in his chair and wears his watch.

Narrative voice: The voice of the character telling the story and relating the incidents.

Patriarchy: A form of social control whereby wealth, property and power belong primarily to men.

Symbolism: A literary technique that confers deeper meaning on objects. For example, Charles wears the gold watch and chain belonging to John Blackwood; here, the symbolic meaning of the watch and chain is in its representation of the patriarchal power Charles hopes to gain.

Analysing a sample topic

'Family is the cause of all the problems in *We Have Always Lived in the Castle.*' Do you agree?

In this topic the statement is very broad, asserting that family causes 'all' the problems in the text. This gives you room to refine the statement according to your understanding of the novel. Family, especially a materialist, patriarchal family, does cause many problems for Merricat, Constance and Uncle Julian, but not all their problems stem from family. Consider the term 'problems', a word you should think carefully about in relation to the novel, which deals with personal and larger societal problems, as well as the familial ones. For example, two other difficulties explored in the text are the small-mindedness of parochial towns and the victimisation of outsiders. Remember to look at the question that follows the statement, in this case 'Do you agree?' You can choose to agree, agree to some extent, or disagree with the statement. In most cases it is better to modify the proposition rather than commit to an 'all or nothing' response. The following sample analysis agrees that family does cause problems but argues that there are also other important sources of conflict in the text.

Sample introduction

> While family does cause many of the problems in *We Have Always Lived in the Castle*, it does not generate all the troubles that the main characters face. Merricat, Constance and, to a certain extent, Uncle Julian, suffered from the challenges of living in John Blackwood's household, and their torment continues when Charles Blackwood arrives. But other difficulties they face are not caused by the Blackwood family, but by society as a whole. Shirley Jackson interrogates family dysfunction in the context of the systemic injustices of patriarchal rule in society, and explores the difficulties of being an outsider in small-town America.

Body paragraph outline

- Family, especially a patriarchal and patrilineal family, assigns indoor, domestic duties to the females and allows the males to control the finances and inherit wealth. John Blackwood ruled his family in this way, as Uncle Julian attests: 'our wives always did as they were told' (p.47). Thomas, the son, would inherit the house and the Blackwood wealth, while Merricat and Constance were expected to modify their behaviour to suit the family, manage the cooking and cleaning, and eventually marry.

- Although Merricat says that the people of the village 'have always hated us' (p.4), the Blackwood family's wealth provided some protection from an antagonistic society. John Blackwood built fences around the property; Mrs Blackwood had social connections to her peers which, in turn, connected the Blackwoods to another part of society. Family provided a buffer from the hostile villagers because 'they were cowards and they were afraid of Blackwoods' (p.7). The villagers were sufficiently intimidated by John Blackwood's money to leave the family unmolested.
- When most of the Blackwood family is poisoned, the remaining Blackwoods are left unprotected from hostile, parochial society. After Constance's trial the intensity of the antagonism increases and the family is further isolated. For example, Merricat reports that 'the Harrises had stopped delivering dairy goods to us six years ago', when the trial took place. In a small town, Merricat, Constance and Uncle Julian are constantly under scrutiny and the subject of gossip, the townspeople 'hating dully and from habit' (p.12).
- Charles gains access to the house because the sisters are really defenceless against claims from the powerful, male-dominated society that assumes women are incompetent. Charles tells them, 'Women alone like you are, you shouldn't keep money in the house'. Similarly, the local Fire Chief, Jim Donell, takes off his official 'Chief' helmet after dousing the fire and becomes the leader of the mob that wrecks the sisters' house.

Sample conclusion

In many ways, the problems of the Blackwood family – its cruelty, power dynamics and assumptions of male superiority – are strongly connected to the wider societal problems of patriarchal rule and small-town narrow-mindedness. Merricat's violent rebellion against her family is insufficient to overcome the problems she and her sister face, since these problems are connected to a wider social malaise.

SAMPLE ANSWER

'The ending of *We Have Always Lived in the Castle* is a victory for Merricat and Constance.' Do you agree?

The resolution of *We Have Always Lived in the Castle* represents a triumph for Merricat and Constance, but in different ways for each character. Their house is ruined and their family is dead but the sisters have gained the freedom to live as they choose, not as they are directed to do. At the end of the novel the Blackwood sisters can claim a victory over the parties who opposed them: their domineering family, Cousin Charles, and the villagers who tried to destroy them. However, it is a victory in a battle that Merricat has designed and waged almost single-handedly, with Constance's wavering support. For Merricat, victory is not a matter of perseverance and self-reliance; she actively fights her enemies and overcomes them. Constance's victory, by contrast, is over her own naivety and malleability. She develops resilience and a growth in understanding through the turmoil she endures.

Merricat and Constance have reason to be aggrieved by their patriarchal and neglectful family. Both sisters suffer oppression from the elder Blackwoods, who live by the precept that 'our wives always did as they were told', and who harshly rebuked any aberrant behaviour. Merricat was 'always in disgrace' and 'a wicked, disobedient child', and this independent spirit led to her parents punishing her with the withdrawal of food and affection. Constance, too, suffers the particularly female punishment of being relegated to the kitchen to cook the family's meals and having to clean the house. In retaliating against the strictures the family imposes on them, Merricat, with Constance's help, wrests power from them by poisoning the whole family, including their younger brother – the male heir, Thomas Blackwood, who would have inherited the house, property and wealth of their father. Consequently, Merricat enables herself and Constance to inherit the house by default, in the absence of any male claim.

This initial victory is threatened by the arrival of the money-hungry Cousin Charles, a member of the extended Blackwood family, who tries to reassert the 'normal' hierarchical order by assuming John Blackwood's role as 'father' of the family, with Constance as wife and Merricat and Uncle Julian as wayward children. Charles undermines their self-sufficiency, telling them that they shouldn't keep money in the house and taking over Merricat's shopping responsibilities; he then threatens Merricat with expulsion from the house with 'come about a month from now, I wonder who *will* still be here? You ... or me?' Merricat goes into battle against the tyrannical Charles, firstly by trying to alert Constance to the threat he represents, telling her, 'Charles is a ghost', then by using Charles' pipe to set fire to the house, forcing him to flee. Charles is, in fact, a 'ghost' of the patriarchal force that she thought she had defeated and Merricat wins her bitter battle with him, at the cost of the burned house.

Jackson's exposé of the unfairness of a woman's place in a patriarchal world culminates in a victory for the sisters at the end of the novel, in that they finally escape the subservient and powerless roles their family has assigned to them. The Blackwood females were consigned to the domestic, internal world of the house, represented by the kitchen, the pantry, the women's china sets and the Dresden figurines in Mrs Blackwood's drawing room. By contrast, the men were free to engage with the political and economic outside world and to order the finances, these roles being represented by the seat at the head of the dining table and John Blackwood's study. However, Merricat, through her extreme actions, rids the house of its male inhabitants and, together with Constance, locks off those parts of the house – the drawing room, dining room and study – that are kept as 'monuments' to the Blackwoods' power. Instead, the sisters live in the highly feminine and functional three remaining rooms – the kitchen, the cellar and the pantry – and here they make a 'castle' of independence.

In their final 'castle' the Blackwood sisters are no longer ridiculed and jeered at by the villagers who ostracised them and later destroyed the contents of their house. Instead, they are feared and propitiated. They live their lives in the domestic heart of the house, reversing the roles of the observer and the observed by peering through the keyhole in the front door to watch the 'strangers' outside. In order to appease the Blackwood sisters, the villagers leave gifts of food and apologies for the harm they have done. Merricat and Constance take on an almost mythological status in their society, sequestered, with their house burned and their belongings destroyed, but having unknown powers. Finally, when Merricat is joined by Constance in their reclusive existence, peering at the 'strangers' through the gap in their front door, they become commentators, rather than merely objects of comment. Imbued with power by the fearful villagers and invisible to them within their castle, their victory in recovering their autonomy is complete.

REFERENCES & READING

Text

Jackson, S 2009, *We Have Always Lived in the Castle*, Penguin Classics. First published in 1962.

References

Abrams, MH & Harpham, GG 2013, *A Glossary of Literary Terms*, 11th edn, Cengage.

Alpha History 2022, 'The Nixon-Khruschev "Kitchen debate" (1959)', https://alphahistory.com/coldwar/nixon-khrushchev-kitchen-debate-1959/

Carpenter, L 1984, 'The Establishment and Preservation of Female Power in Shirley Jackson's *We Have Always Lived in the Castle*', *Frontiers: A Journal of Womens Studies*, vol. 8, no. 1, pp.32–8.

Franklin, R 2016, *Shirley Jackson: A Rather Haunted Life,* W W Norton & Company, New York.

Gilbert, S & Gubar, S 1979, *The Madwoman in the Attic,* Yale University Press, New Haven.

Hague, A 2005, 'A Faithful Anatomy of Our Times: Reassessing Shirley Jackson', *Frontiers: A Journal of Women Studies*, vol. 26, no. 2, pp. 73–96.

Heller, Z 2016, 'The Haunted Mind of Shirley Jackson', *The New Yorker*, 17 October.

Rubenstein, R 1996, 'House Mothers and Haunted Daughters: Shirley Jackson and Female Gothic', *Tulsa Studies in Women's Literature*, vol. 15, no. 2, pp.309–31.

Woodruff, SC 1967, 'The Real Horror Elsewhere', *Southwest Review*, vol. 52, no. 2, pp.152–62.